Image Before My Eyes

Image Before My Eyes

A Photographic History of Jewish Life in Poland Before the Holocaust

LUCJAN DOBROSZYCKI and BARBARA KIRSHENBLATT-GIMBLETT

SCHOCKEN BOOKS, NEW YORK

Published in cooperation with YIVO Institute for Jewish Research

Library of Congress Cataloging-in-Publication Data

Dobroszycki, Lucjan.
Image before my eyes : a photographic history of Jewish life in
Poland before the Holocaust / Lucjan Dobroszycki and Barbara
Kirshenblatt-Gimblett.
p.   cm.
Published in cooperation with the YIVO Institute for Jewish
Research. Includes bibliographical references and indexes.
ISBN 0-8052-1026-1
1. Jews—Poland—History—19th century. 2. Jews—Poland—
History—20th century. 3. Jews—Poland—Pictorial works.
4. Poland—Ethnic relations. 5. Poland—Pictorial works.
I. Kirshenblatt-Gimblett, Barbara. II. Title.
DS135.P6D62   1995
943.8′004924—dc20   94-26783

TYPOGRAPHIC DESIGN BY HERMANN STROHBACH

NOTE: The romanization of Yiddish in this volume follows the
transliteration-transcription system of the Library of Congress, the
YIVO Institute for Jewish Research, and Uriel Weinreich, *Modern
English-Yiddish Yiddish-English Dictionary* (New York, 1968).
Accordingly, only names and the first word of Yiddish titles are
capitalized.

IN MEMORY

OF THE DESTROYED

JEWISH COMMUNITIES

OF POLAND

ACKNOWLEDGMENTS

This volume could not have been completed without the expert assistance and constant support of the staff of the YIVO Institute for Jewish Research and the Max Weinreich Center for Advanced Jewish Studies. Dr. Marvin I. Herzog and Dr. Isaiah Trunk read the entire manuscript at each stage of its preparation and made invaluable comments.

Dr. Dan Miron kindly provided the material for the section on literature, and Dr. Nahma Sandrow generously allowed us to use the manuscript of her volume *Vagabond Stars: A World History of the Yiddish Theater* (Harper & Row, 1977) as a basis for the section on theater. David Rogow, Dr. Mordkhe Schaechter, Beatrice Silverman Weinreich, and the late Szymon Dawidowicz, Rachel Erlich and Dr. Shlomo Noble answered innumerable questions and shared their intimate knowledge of Jewish culture and the Yiddish language. Dr. Jacob Goldberg of the Hebrew University made valuable comments on portions of the manuscript when he visited YIVO.

We are deeply grateful to the indefatigable staff of the YIVO library and archives—Dina Abramowicz, Marek Web, Bella Weinberg, Zalman Alpert, and Chil Romanowicz—who not only helped us to locate important materials but also provided assistance with problems of translation and transliteration-transcription. Chaim Bolek Ellenbogen was always ready to lend a hand with many technical problems.

Suzanna Fogel, who for five years helped Dr. Lucjan Dobroszycki catalogue the photograph collection, assisted with all the aspects of the preparation of the volume. Toby Blum Dobkin, Mark Friedman, and Isaiah Kuperstein, Fellows of the Max Weinreich Center for Advanced Jewish Studies, gathered material for the bibliography. Irena Zabłudowska helped prepare the charts and Sandra Lundy located materials in various New York libraries.

With endless patience, Raisle Goldstein and the late Luba Condell typed the munuscript and handled with extraordinary expertise the many problems wrought by foreign language terms in the text.

To Stuart Silver, then Head of Design at the Metropolitan Museum of Art, we owe very special thanks. He worked closely with us in the initial stages and designed the exhibition of these photographs, which was organized by the YIVO and held at The Jewish Museum in 1976. This exhibition was made possible through the generous grants of the National Endowment for the Humanities, the New York State Council on the Arts, and the Memorial Foundation for Jewish Culture.

The late Clare Herzog, who applied her intellectual acumen and editorial expertise to shape the text as she worked with us on the exhibition, left her deep imprint on this volume as well. We owe her our greatest debt of gratitude.

Many organizations, libraries, and archives have, through their warm cooperation and generosity, greatly contributed to YIVO's collection of photographs, which forms the basis for both the exhibition and this volume. We are grateful to the Bund Archives of the Jewish Labor Movement (New York), the American Joint Distribution Committee, the Hebrew Immigrant Aid Society (HIAS), the Józef Piłsudski Institute of America, the Royal Library of Copenhagen, the American Jewish Archives (Cincinnati), *The Jewish Daily Forward* (New York), the Archives of *Der tog* (New York).

With a full awareness of the historical and cultural value of their personal memorabilia, thousands of individuals entrusted their family snapshots and albums to the YIVO, where they are preserved for posterity. It is thanks to them that YIVO was able to amass the fullest photographic record of Jewish life in Poland in the world.

We are deeply grateful to the late Shmuel Lapin, Executive Secretary of YIVO when the volume was in preparation, who initiated this project in 1970. During the seven years that this project was in the making, the late Hannah Fryshdorf, former Assistant Director of YIVO, encouraged this project and did all in her power to create the best working conditions and atmosphere. Steeped in Polish Jewish culture, she offered us her insights and sensibility as one who experienced the life captured in the photographs.

Finally, we must thank our families—Felicja and Joanna Dobroszycki and Maxwell Gimblett—for their unflagging moral support and patience.

CONTENTS

Part Four

Creating a Modern Existence   153

Appendixes   251

Index of Names   265

Index of Places   268

Introduction

Polish Jewry, once the largest Jewish community in Europe, constituted a world center of Jewish cultural creativity for centuries. The thousand-year history of this community is exceptionally well documented. The traditional resources of the historian—written sources, archeological remains, art, and architecture—were supplemented in the mid-nineteenth century with the advent of photography, which introduced both a radically new kind of visual image and a new type of historical document.

The hundreds of thousands of images that were created by means of the camera not only captured major historical events and important personages but also immortalized the intimate details and humblest aspects of everyday life. This very profusion of photographs, of visual eyewitness accounts taken in innumerable places and situations, has made it possible to reconstruct in great detail the social and cultural ambiance of an era as it was seen by those who lived through it. But in order to accomplish this, the cultural historian must reckon with the paradox that "before a photograph can be accepted as a document, it must itself be documented,"* as Beaumont Newhall has stated.

Though the camera does not lie, the photograph is neither value free nor does it provide more than a desituated fragment, accidentally preserved through time, of a larger picture. As John Szarkowski has remarked, "To quote out of context is the essence of the photographer's craft."† One important way of compensating for the fragmentary character of the single photograph is to place it in the frame of reference provided by a large collection of related images and to gloss it on the basis of the materials conventionally used by the historian and the ethnographer. This is what we have attempted to do in this photographic history of Jewish life in Poland.

The ten thousand photographs in the Polish collection at

---

*Beaumont Newhall, *The History of Photography from 1839 to the Present Day,* 4th ed., revised and enlarged (New York: Museum of Modern Art and George Eastman House, 1964), p. 150.
†John Szarkowski, *The Photographer's Eye* (New York: Museum of Modern Art, 1966), p. 70.

the YIVO Institute for Jewish Research form the basis both for this album and for the exhibition that the YIVO organized and presented at the Jewish Museum in New York City in 1976. Three hundred photographs have been selected, documented, and arranged to provide moving testimony to the modern Jewish experience in Poland before World War II. The period documented by the photographs was a time of social experimentation and struggle, creativity, and intense interaction of Jews with the surrounding multiethnic society.

Presentations on East European Jewry have often been nostalgic and have dwelled upon the themes of Jewish piety and isolation, poverty, and persecution. They have also treated the East European Jewish community as historically, geographically, and culturally undifferentiated. In contrast, this volume offers a fresh approach. The camera becomes a chronicler of major historical events and their impact on the Polish Jewish community, as distinct from East European Jewry as a whole. The result is an eyewitness pictorial account of the confrontation of Polish Jewry with modernity—documenting its involvement in Polish society, its political and cultural movements, educational and religious institutions, the quality of Jewish life in the great urban centers of Poland, theater and cinema, intellectual and literary activities, and music and sports.

The photographs presented here span a seventy-five year period. Our first photograph is a portrait taken in 1864 of Hirsh and Hinde Poznański, an elegantly attired couple from Włocławek, a small town on the banks of the Vistula River. Our last photograph was taken on September 1, 1939, the day that marks the beginning of World War II and the annihilation of Polish Jewry: it shows a train that carries German soldiers and bears the slogan "Wir fahren nach Polen um Juden zu versohlen" ("We are riding to Poland to beat up the Jews.").

At the time when the Poznańskis had their picture taken, Poland did not exist as a political entity, for from 1795 until 1918, when the Second Polish Republic was established, Poland was divided among Russia, Prussia, and Austria. As a

Hirsh and Hinde Poznański.
Włocławek, 1864.
Forward Art Section,
November 4, 1934

result of frequent changes of boundaries, the geographical territory designated by the term Poland varies by historical period. In this volume, Poland is defined in terms of the boundaries of the Second Polish Republic that were in effect from 1921 until 1939. Photographs from this geographical area are included regardless of when they were taken and regardless of the political administration of the period. For example, our photographs from the city of Vilna were taken during the periods when the city was under various administrations—Russian Empire, German authorities during World War I, Independent Lithuanian Republic, and Second Polish Republic. The history of Poland's changing boundaries may be seen on the accompanying maps.

This volume, which opens with a history of Jewish photography in Poland as seen through the YIVO's collection, is

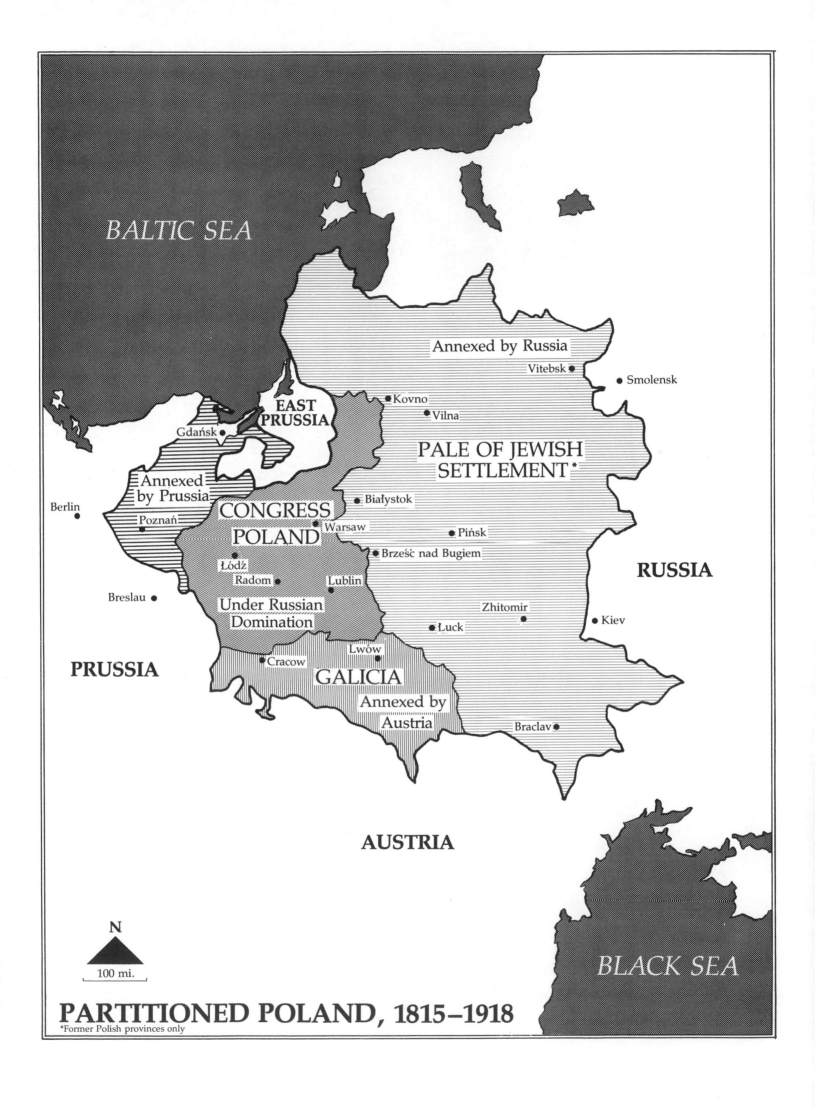

BALTIC SEA

Annexed by Russia

Vitebsk •
• Smolensk

EAST
PRUSSIA

• Kovno

Gdańsk • • Vilna

PALE OF JEWISH
SETTLEMENT *

Annexed
by Prussia

Berlin
•
Poznań •

CONGRESS

POLAND

• Białystok

Warsaw

RUSSIA

Łódź
Radom •

• Pińsk

• Brześć nad Bugiem

Breslau •

Under Russian
Domination

Lublin •

• Zhitomir

• Kiev

Cracow •

Lwów •

GALICIA

• Łuck

PRUSSIA

Annexed by
Austria

• Braclav

AUSTRIA

N

100 mi.

BLACK SEA

PARTITIONED POLAND, 1815–1918
*Former Polish provinces only

BALTIC SEA

LATVIA

LITHUANIA

Niemen

Niemenczyn

Nowa-Wilejka

Vilna Smorgonie

EAST PRUSSIA
(GERMANY)

Wołożyn

Jeziory

Gdańsk

Grodno

Lubcza

Grajewo

Mir

Nowogródek

Łomża

Wołpa

Wołkowysk

Białystok

Świsłocz

Baranowicze

Bydgoszcz

Mława

Zabłudów

Vistula

Długosiodło Brańsk

Włocławek

Nowe Miasto

Orla

Szereszów

Dobrzyń nad Wisłą

Płońsk

Nasielsk

Wysokie Litewskie

Drohiczyn

Łachwa

Poznań

Gąbin

Wołomin

Bug

Zbąszyn

Żychlin

Jabłonna

Pińsk

Warta

Skierniewice

Warsaw

Miedzeszyn

Mińsk Mazowiecki

Brześć nad Bugiem

Wysock

Brzeziny

Otwock

Kalisz

Łódź

Góra Kalwaria

Prypeć

Łaskarzew

Maciejowice

Klesów

Łask

Przytyk

Dęblin

Wąwolnica

Przysucha

Radom

Chełm

Włoszczowa

Szydłowiec

Lublin

Łuck

Równe

Kielce

Kazimierz nad Wisłą

Jeziorany Żydowskie

GERMANY

Częstochowa

Annopol

Hrubieszów

Ostróg

Bogorja

Zamość

Krzemieniec

Staszów

Brody

Katowice

Pacanów

Cracow

Żabno

Biała

Tarnów

Lwów

Tarnopol

U.S.S.R.

Bobowa

Krynica Zdrój

Chodorów

Drohobycz

Rohatyn

Stryj

Czortków

Stanisławów

Rosochacz

Zaleszczyki

CZECHOSLOVAKIA

Dniestr

Kosów

RUMANIA

Oder

N

100 mi.

THE SECOND POLISH REPUBLIC 1921–1939

divided into three major sections. In the first part, entitled "Persistence of the Past," the photographs demonstrate the ongoing vitality of traditional lifestyles. As Szarkowski has written, "Photographs stand in a special relation to time, for they describe only the present";* but to the extent that the past continues to be part of the present, the photograph can capture it as well. Thanks to the photographers whose interests were historical, ethnographic, or antiquarian we have a very full visual record of old settlements, their architecture and cemeteries, and the folkways of their inhabitants.

The second unit, "The Camera as Chronicler," covers a period of political struggle and Jewish involvement in it from Czarist times to the eve of World War II—the Revolution of 1905, the First World War and the German occupation, the formation of the Second Polish Republic and the Polish-Russian War of 1920, emigration to America and Palestine, the pogroms of the 1930s, the Zbąszyn Affair and *Kristallnacht*, and Poland's preparations for the German invasion. Genuine news photographs obtained by the Jewish press from news agencies and correspondents, the photographic records made by the occupying forces and by Jewish relief organizations, as well as the memorabilia of Jewish revolutionaries, soldiers, and political and communal leaders provide the basis for this chronicle.

The last and largest section is called "Creating a Modern Existence" and reveals the full spectrum of Jewish activities in urban centers, the quality of middle-class life, the vigor of social and political movements and parties, the role of Jewish communal organizations, and the activities of scholars, writers, theater people, filmmakers, and athletes. Statistical and toponymic information is provided in the Appendix.

This photographic history of Jewish life in Poland is intended to give the reader a glimpse of the richness and vitality of life in the largest Jewish community in Europe as it was before it was destroyed.

*Szarkowski, p. 100.

Part One
A History of Jewish Photography in Poland

In 1839, the year Daguerre announced his invention of photography to the world, a daguerreotype was brought to Warsaw, where it was advertised for sale for the fantastic sum of one thousand złotys. The next year, Daguerre's *History and Process of Photogenic Drawing by Means of Daguerreotype* was translated into Polish, and by 1847, Moritz Scholz had established the first daguerreotype studio in Poland. Fifteen years later, in 1862, there were thirty-three photography studios in Warsaw alone.

Among the earliest studios was that of Karol Beyer (1818–1877). The father of Polish photography, he introduced the collodian process and the collotype into Poland. Beyer was in Paris at the time Daguerre's invention was made public and was in London a decade later, when Frederich Scott Archer invented the collodian process for making negatives. In Munich, he studied with Joseph Albert, inventor of the collotype process for printing photographs.

A Jewish photographer who pioneered in the development of photography in Poland was Maksymilian Fajans (1827–1890). A draftsman, lithographer, and photographer, Fajans graduated from the Warsaw School of Fine Arts. He was studying color lithography in Paris with R. J. Lemercière when Daguerre's work was first made known. When Fajans returned to Warsaw in the early fifties, he opened his own lithography shop and photography studio (which was still functioning at the turn of the century under the name of Leonard) and traveled around the countryside doing landscape photography. The first in Warsaw to make color lithographs, he specialized in reproducing works of art and was a contributor of photographs to *Kłosy*, an early illustrated magazine in partitioned Poland.

Fajans won gold medals for his photographs in Warsaw, St. Petersburg, and London, and a bronze medal in the General Exhibition in Paris in 1867. His studio was attended by the most prominent people, among them Nasredin, the Shah of Iran, who had his portrait made by Fajans in 1880, while visiting Warsaw. The Shah later wrote that "my portrait was pre-

Carte de visite made by R. Major-kiewicz in the 1860s.

This advertisement for one of the oldest Jewish photography studios in partitioned Poland appears in Russian, Polish, and Yiddish in M. Spektor's *Varshaver familyen-kalendar 5654/1893–1894: a bukh far literatur un gezelshaft mit anonsn in farsheydene shprakhn* and reads as follows:

> The thirty-five-year-old photography studio of R. Majorkiewicz in Warsaw, 3 Krasiński Square, near the park, does everything in the photography line beautifully and inexpensively. Orders are promptly and perfectly done. For every dozen *cartes de visite*, one fancy *cabinet portrait* will be given away free.

Carte de visite made by Leonard and Company, formerly M. Fajans Studio, in Warsaw.

viously taken in St. Petersburg but the photograph made in Warsaw turned out much better, for the Warsaw photographers are famous throughout Europe."* Fajans's last and greatest work was the *Album of Landmarks* (1873–1883).

Like Beyer and Fajans, many of the early photographers working in Poland had been trained as printers and artists and had learned the photography trade abroad, and were involved in developing methods of reproducing photographs and works of art in magazines and books (and later on postcards) at the same time that they were perfecting the techniques of photography proper. Thus the first photography manual written in Polish was published during the same year (1859) that photographs were reproduced in the first illustrated Polish magazine *(Tygodnik Ilustrowany)*. In the 1880s, magazines devoted exclusively to the techniques and art of photography were initiated in Warsaw and Lwów—*Polski Przegląd Fotograficzny* and *Światło*, among others.

The artistic training of these early photographers, who had a penchant for naming their studios after such great painters as Rembrandt and Raphael, is evident in their approach to portrait photography, which they modeled on portrait painting. Most of the nineteenth-century photographs in the YIVO collection are studio portraits, the stock-in-trade of the early photographers. Indeed, our earliest photograph of a Polish Jew is a daguerreotype portrait of Dr. Isaac Erter, a distinguished Hebrew satirist in Galicia. The portrait was probably made in 1848 by the Miethke and Wawra studio in Vienna, where Erter participated in the election of Noah Manheimer to the Parliament. Portraits appearing after his death on postcards and in books were probably made from this daguerreotype.

The disadvantages of the daguerreotype method, which produced only one positive image with each exposure, were overcome by photographs in the form of the *carte de visite* (calling card), patented by André Disderi in France in 1855,

*Wacław Żdżarski, *Historia fotografii warszawskiej* (Warsaw: Państwowe Wydawnictwo Naukowe, 1974), pp. 63–64.

Daguerreotype of Dr. Isaac Erter
made by the Miethke and Wawra
Studio in Vienna in 1848.

Postcard of Dr. Isaac Erter (1791–1851),
with the following inscription in Hebrew:

> Born in a village in Galicia, he was a satiric
> writer of the Haskalah period. During his
> lifetime his works were read with pleasure
> and he was acknowledged as a distin-
> guished writer. He was considered a master
> of style and was noted for his florid prose
> and satiric wit. He was the editor of *He-
> Halutz.* His writings were collected in *The
> Watchman of the House of Israel* in 1858.

Seen here are the symbols conventionally
used on postcards of writers— the lute or
harp, the feather pen and inkwell, the
weighty tomes, and the Jugendstil frame.
Postcard: Verlags-Buchhandlung A. Robinsohn, Stanisławów

Cartes de visite made in the oldest Polish and Jewish photography studios in partitioned Poland. Actual size of photographs is about 2½″ × 3¾″.

A HISTORY OF JEWISH PHOTOGRAPHY
IN POLAND

Cabinets Portraits. The actual size of photographs is about 5½″ × 4¼″.

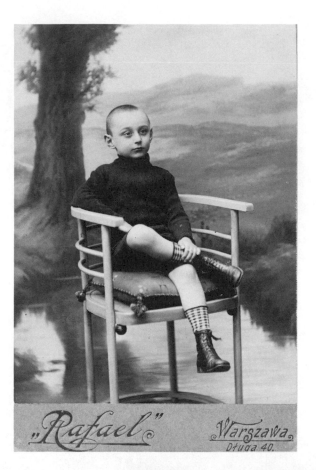

and the larger *cabinet portrait*, introduced in England in 1866. Jan Mieczkowski, a Polish painter and traveling daguèrreotypist, studied in Germany, from whence he brought the *carte de visite* to Poland during the late 1850s. An astute businessman, he opened a very successful studio in Warsaw in 1857, and in a single year sold 237,000 *carte de visite* mounts to photographers all over Poland.

The *carte de visite* and *cabinet portrait* continued to be the favorite formats for portraits in Poland well into the twentieth century. The subjects are generally dressed in their best, sometimes borrowed for the occasion, and in keeping with the vogue bear a rather stern expression as they maintain a stylized pose in an elegant, often fanciful, painted setting. Special artists were employed to construct the props—the painted backdrop of a landscape or luxurious interior, a tree stump or column or balustrade, some drapery—and to arrange the pose. The earliest such portraits in our collection, which are from the 1860s and 1870s, reflect the elegance of an affluent elite.

Group portrait, taken outdoors by A. Osiecki, a traveling photographer. Żychlin, ca: 1904. A cloth backdrop hides most of the fence and simulates an elegant interior setting in this remote little town. In all probability the dog belonged to the photographer and was one of his standard props.

A drive in the country without leaving the photographer's studio. Warsaw, 1910. *Forward* Art Section, March 24, 1935

Studio portrait of Yudl Ajdelman in Świsłocz, 1911. The bicycle wheels are held together with wire, a sign that the bicycle has been retired from active service and is strictly a photographer's prop. Avrom Ain Collection

The wealthy subjects of so many of the early portraits had sought out and paid handsomely for the services of the artistic studio photographers. In contrast, ethnographically-oriented photographers like Michał Greim left their studios to wander through small villages and towns, where they recorded the traditional way of life conserved there. They also brought photogenic "types" back to the studio, where they arranged them in artistic poses and *tableaux vivants*, depicting such familiar scenes as children studying in a *kheyder* (traditional Jewish primary school). These *tableaux vivants* became a favorite subject of later postcards.

Michał Greim (1828–1911) was a printer by trade and for twenty years managed the government printing house in Kamenets Podolsk, in the Ukraine. He was a passionate collector of old coins, books, and artifacts, and was one of the first to photograph traditional Jewish life. In 1860, he opened a photography studio in Kamenets Podolsk and at this time made friends with Karol Beyer, who shared his numismatic and antiquarian interests and his involvement in photography and printing. Together they pioneered in the development in

Photographs taken by Michał Greim in Volhynia and Podolia between 1860 and 1880, and presented to Eliza Orzeszkowa in 1891, with his own captions.

"Going to sell liquor and, if possible, to smuggle some."

"A plague! The local people call him shabby, a buyer of clothes left by the dead. He is also called a courtyard jackal. He can foresee who is about to die, since 'Whoever is sick is sure to die.'"

"Kheyder," a *tableau vivant*.

Strassenhändler.   הרוכל.

№ 49   חברת "לבנון"

Street pedlar. Posed studio photographs of traditional "types" were a popular subject of Jewish postcards. Photographer: M. Nappelbaum/Postcard: Lebanon Society

Poland of photomechanical methods of printing. Greim, who acquired a reputation as an excellent photographer of anthropological and historical subjects, published some of his photographs in albums and was a contributor to *Kłosy*. He received a silver medal in 1900 for an exhibition in Warsaw of thirty collotypes of the life of various ethnic groups in the rural areas of Podolia and Volhynia and was honored by the Cracow Academy of Science and the Imperial Academy of Ethnography in St. Petersburg for his work.

In 1891, Greim sent one hundred and sixty photographs of life in Podolia and Volhynia to the Polish author Eliza Orzeszkowa in honor of the fifty years she had been active in the literary field. The collection, which he dedicated to her in verse, included twenty-three photographs of Jews taken as early as 1860. His intimate knowledge of the local people and their culture is apparent both in the photographs and in the captions, which are often poetic, whimsical, or satirical, as was the style in popular photography in the nineteenth and early twentieth centuries.

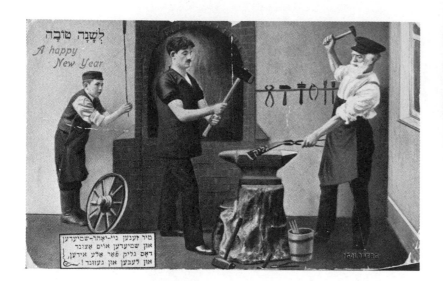

Two allegorical Jewish New Year's greeting postcards. The smith is forging a
piece of metal inscribed with the word *glik* (good fortune). The verse reads as
follows:

> We are New Year blacksmiths
> And we are now forging
> Good fortune, life, and health
> For all Jews.

Postcard: Bukhhandlung "Alt-nay-land," Warsaw

God's angel contemplates the heavenly book in which each person's deeds
and fate for the coming year have been recorded. The verse reads as follows:

> God's angel sits over the Book of Memories,
> Reviews the good deeds, contemplates the transgressions,
> Soon he exclaims with joy, "Not bad!
> There is not a single wicked person among the Jews,
> Not even one guilty one. In short, a people worthy of salvation,
> A people that should and ought to have good fortune
> And be sent thousands of blessings from heaven."

Postcard: Verlag S. Resnik, Warsaw

Postcards. Tens of thousands of postcards on Jewish subjects were issued in
Poland by commercial publishers as well as by Jewish social and political organizations. Such firms as Jehudia, S. Resnik, Lebanon Society, and Central issued
only Jewish cards. A. Robinsohn, W. Borkowski, Artysty, A. Fialko, A. Wizun,
"Ruch," Wydawnictwo Salon Malarzy Polskich, and others issued postcards on
other subjects as well. Many of the postcards published in Poland were actually
printed in Germany, the center of postcard printing before World War I.

Jewish postcards covered a wide variety of subjects. Entire series were devoted to Jewish writers, political figures, old Jewish residential areas, syna-

gogues, hospitals, schools, ceremonial art, modern painting and sculpture, and traditional types and scenes.

One of the earliest and most popular Jewish postcard genres is the greeting card for the Jewish New Year. Extant Jewish New Year's cards date from the early nineteenth century in Germany; the first to appear in postcard form date from the last quarter of the nineteenth century. Holidays, customs, and conventional scenes from Jewish life are frequently depicted on these cards as are Biblical scenes, moralistic allegories, and humorous and sentimental subjects. On some cards, the New Year's greeting appears in the form of a popular verse. On a number of cards, the greeting *leshono toyvo* ("for a good year") has been applied to the face of the card with a rubber stamp. The greeting is an abbreviated form of the traditional formula "May you be inscribed and sealed [in the Book of Life] for a good year."

Postcards on Jewish subjects were made from photographs and from drawings, graphics, and paintings. The negatives were often heavily retouched and sometimes there was even paint over the print itself. Imitating the pictorial effects of paintings, the photographic postcards often showed a *tableau vivant* of costumed and posed models in a theatrical or fanciful setting.

During the last quarter of the nineteenth century, portrait photography served the first scholars concerned with the physical anthropology of Jews. One of the most distinguished of these was Samuel Weissenberg (1867–1928), a medical doctor in Elisavetgrad, Ukraine, whose work *Die südrussischen Juden: eine anthropometrische Studie* (1895) won the gold medal from the Moscow Society for Natural Sciences. A first-rate ethnographer and folklorist, Weissenberg published numerous articles and photographs of Jewish folkways in *Globus* and other illustrated journals at the turn of the century. He traveled widely, and the photographs he took also served others researching the physical anthropology of Jews, most notably Maurice Fishberg (1872–1934), anthropological consultant to the United States Bureau of Immigration. Arthur Ruppin (1876–1943), founder of the modern sociology of the Jews, illustrated his discussion of physical anthropology with photographs he had himself taken as well as with portrait photographs of Polish Jews culled from the rotogravure Art Section of the *Jewish Daily Forward,* published in New York.

Historians of Jewish art and architecture found the camera to be an invaluable tool in their research. Such a pioneer as

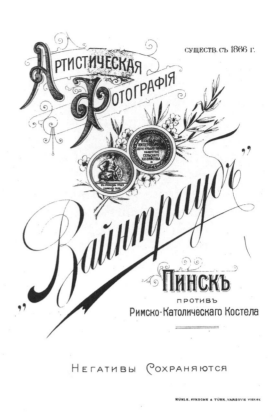

Photographic reproduction of an eighteenth-century painting of a woman wearing a jeweled headcovering *(shterntikhl)*. The Weintraub studio in Pińsk, where the photograph was made, was established in 1866. It specialized in the photography of art objects of Jewish interest. Information about the studio is on the back of the photograph. Paul S. Lourie Collection

Matthias Bersohn (1823–1908), a historian and collector of Polish and Jewish antiquities and art, was the first to photograph systematically wooden synagogues, the subject of several studies he made. The Warsaw Jewish community established the Bersohn Museum of Jewish Antiquities to house the collection he bequeathed to them.

Majer Bałaban (1877–1942), an eminent Jewish historian in Poland, expanded on the pioneering efforts of Bersohn. He illustrated his many studies with hundreds of photographs he had taken of Jewish environs, landmarks, architecture, tombstones, and artifacts. He was a founder and director of the Institute for Jewish Studies (Warsaw) and patronized an association of Jewish students—the Lovers of Antiquities—whose goal was to preserve Jewish culture "by photographing the historical remains, which are being lost irretrievably every day." Szymon Zajczyk, one of Bałaban's students at the University of Warsaw, used his photographic expertise to further his research on wooden synagogues and became the leading scholar on the subject.

Ethnographers first made full use of the camera at the beginning of the twentieth century. The earliest ethnographic expedition to study Jewish life in Eastern Europe had been organized in the 1850s by M. Berlin, member of the Imperial Russian Geographical Society; and individuals had traveled and, to a limited extent, had photographed Jewish folkways throughout the latter half of the nineteenth century. However, it was not until the expedition organized by S. An-ski in 1912 that a team of scholars systematically recorded Jewish folkways with the help of the camera and cylinder recorder. An-ski, a Yiddish belletrist, playwright, and folklorist, was spon-

Zusman Kisselhof (b. ca. 1874), on the S. An-ski ethnographic expedition to Volhynia and Podolia, seen here making sound recordings of Jewish folklore. Kisselhof was a teacher and musician who collected and arranged Yiddish folksongs.

Rabbi Yehude Leyb Złotnik (b. 1887), one of the founders of the Mizrachi (Orthodox Zionist) movement in Poland, writer, and folklorist. Under the pen name Yehude Elzet, he published important compendia of Yiddish sayings and customs. *Forward* Collection

Shmuel Lehman, recording folklore in Warsaw, 1931. Lehman is known for his unique collections of folklore from and about the Jewish underworld, especially Yiddish songs and tales about thieves. Studio: Kuder

sored by the Jewish Historic-Ethnographic Society in St. Petersburg and was funded by Baron Horace Günzburg to organize an ethnographic expedition into the region where Michał Greim had taken photographs half a century earlier. In the remote villages and towns of Volhynia and Podolia, an area of dense Jewish settlement, traditional folkways were well preserved. It was here that Hasidism had emerged. The expedition succeeded in gathering and taking more than two thousand photographs in addition to collecting artifacts, manuscripts, communal record books, and to recording in writing and on cylinders thousands of Yiddish folktales, folksongs, riddles, proverbs, and folk beliefs. The expedition was cut short by the outbreak of World War I.

During the first three years of the Great War, all of partitioned Poland was occupied by the German army. For thousands of German soldiers, officers, civilians, and newsmen, Poland was not only a conquest but also an exotic and fascinating country, which they had never seen before and which would never be the same again because of the radical changes that their very presence had brought about. The perception of these outsiders, very few of them professional photographers, can be seen in the thousands of snapshots, albums,

Taking a group photograph in Łódź at the start of the German occupation in 1915. Individual portraits were cut out of the photo and attached to the identity cards required by the German authorities. Gustav Eisner Collection

postcards, and news photographs that they produced during and after the war as a record and souvenir of their visit. A typical album, *Zwischen Styr und Bug*, includes panoramas of villages and rural landscapes in each season, shots of thatch-roofed dwellings, villagers in their folk costumes, street scenes, the well and water mill, the town square, market and church, domestic life and interiors, subsistence farming, traditional crafts, and the daily life of German soldiers in their military installations. "Jüdische Typen" are included among the "Volks-typen."

World War I was not the first armed conflict to be recorded by the camera. This distinction is reserved for the Crimean War, which was photographed by Roger Fenton in 1855. However, the early documentary photographers were limited in their ability to capture action by the bulkiness of their cameras, the heavy glass plates, the slow lenses that required long exposures, and other technical problems. Nonetheless, many of their documentary photographs were among the first news photographs, even though they were not used in newspapers until later. A major factor that made the routine use of photographs in the newspapers possible was the development of techniques for using a standard press for printing photographs together with type directly on newsprint. Most important was the half-tone process invented in the 1880s and refined in the decades following.

The Jewish press first emerged in Eastern Europe during the beginning of the nineteenth century, publishing in Hebrew, Yiddish, Russian, Polish, and German. Most of the periodicals were short-lived. Only after the Revolution of 1905, when Czarist censorship was temporarily relaxed, were daily newspapers with large circulations established, the two most important being the Yiddish dailies *Haynt* and *Der moment*. Photographs were first used, albeit sporadically, in the Jewish press in partitioned Poland in the 1890s. But it was not until World War I that photographs were widely used, and then primarily in illustrated weekly supplements and special illustrated periodicals.

Among the first Jewish periodicals in partitioned Poland to print photographs were M. Spektor's *Warsaw Jewish Family Calendar 5654 (1893/1894): A Book for Literature and Society with Notices in Various Languages* and *The Jewish Folk Calendar 1899/1900*, published in Lwów. These almanacs, which are in Yiddish, used only two or three drawings and photographs. During the first decades of the twentieth century, although drawings continued to be used, photographs appeared with greater regularity, and their range was extended beyond portraits to include landmarks and public events. Thus, in 1903–1904, *Hatzefira* (which began as a Hebrew language weekly in 1862 and became a daily in 1886) published photographs of the funeral of Dr. Theodor Herzl, of synagogues and cemeteries, and of Marie and Pierre Curie in their laboratory. In 1910, *Izraelita*, a Jewish Polish-language weekly, printed a special issue in honor of Eliza Orzeszkowa, illustrated with photographs of her. In 1911, *Der shtral*, a Yiddish weekly issued in Warsaw, printed four photographs of a clash between police and anarchists in London; these were among the earliest genuine news photographs used in the Jewish press in partitioned Poland.

Two of the first Jewish periodicals in partitioned Poland to advertise themselves as illustrated magazines were *Di mode: a ilustrirter modn-zhurnal un familyen-blat* (Fashion: An Illustrated Fashion Magazine and Family Paper), established in 1906 in Vilna, and *Roman-tsaytung: a ilustrirtes vokhnblat far literatur, kunst, un visnshaft* (Novel Journal: Illustrated Weekly for Literature, Art, and Scholarship), which was initiated in 1907 in Warsaw, and which claimed to be the first such publication. *Di mode* had included in its first issue a few photographs of hair styles and many drawings of the latest fashions in Berlin and Paris. Anticipating the scope of the later illustrated magazines, *Roman-tsaytung* announced in its first issue that it would publish "illustrations and pictures of the most important events, which every reader will find of interest." This included everything from photographs of the presidium of the Eighth Zionist Congress and of women in government positions, to shots of the construction of a forty-seven story building in the United States.

It was only after World War I, however, that illustrated magazines used photographs on almost every page, achieved a higher quality of reproduction, and covered the widest range of subjects. Accordingly, in 1919, the front page of the first issue of *Ilustrirte velt: vokhn-zhurnal far literatur, kunst, un kultur-fragen* (Illustrated World: Weekly Journal for Literature, Art, and Cultural Affairs) featured a photograph entitled "The Masters of the World," which shows President Wilson, Lloyd George, Georges Clemenceau, and Vittorio Emanuele Orlando at the Versailles Peace Conference. In 1923, at the height of the depreciation of the Polish mark, *Ilustrirte vokh: zhurnal far vort un bild* (Illustrated Week: Journal for Word and Picture) was established with difficulty; the price of one copy, which should have been one or two Polish marks, was one million marks. In a special issue published December 4, 1927, "Fifty Numbers of *Ilustrirte vokh*: Our Holiday–Your Holiday," the editor states:

> *Our path was difficult, truly very difficult, without capital, even without the understanding of those who can and should support such an enterprise. Almost empty-handed we issued one number after another. Intoxicated by this fine achievement and by your loyalty, readers, we, the humble group of founders and builders of the* Ilustrirte vokh, *with the greatest abandon, shook ourselves free of the nonbelievers and boldly strode forward as we noted that the* Ilustrirte vokh *appeared regularly in the waiting rooms of Jewish doctors, engineers, and lawyers, that the assimilated Jewish woman sits in the Polish theater with the* Ilustrirte vokh *and is not ashamed to leaf through the aesthetic Yiddish printed pages freely and openly. . . . The Jewish newspaper kiosk has now acquired a European look. . . . We have given the Yiddish reader the courage to demand that what appears in other languages also be made available in Yiddish.*

The major sections of *Ilustrirte vokh* were news of the week, the Jewish world, poetry and prose, exhibitions, travel, theater and film, social events, woman's world, beauty contests (for example, the most beautiful Jewish child in Poland), sports,

1 The front page of the first issue (May 17, 1907) of *Roman-tsaytung: a ilustrirtes vokhnblat far literatur, kunst, un visnshaft* features a photograph of Leopold Demuth as Alfio in the opera *Cavalleria Rusticana*.

2 "The greatest Jewish strongman—the modern Samson." On February 19, 1925, *Ilustrirte vokh* announced the coming performance of Zishe Breitbart: "The wonderman, about whom the whole world talks and the newspapers write. His power has created great excitement in all of Europe. He is currently the greatest attraction in Berlin. He will soon be in Warsaw."

Zishe Breitbart (1887–1925) was born in Łódź, the son of a blacksmith. Shortly after his Warsaw appearance, he died of a wound suffered during a performance in the circus arena.

chess, and children's world. The subjects of articles and photoessays ranged from a Samaritan Passover to topless dancers of the Folies Bergère, from a Purim masquerade ball to moon shots from the Wilson observatory in London. Of special interest are a review of an exhibition of landscape photographs in Warsaw and an article on nude photography as an art form.

Veltshpigl (World Mirror), an illustrated monthly sent free of charge to the subscribers of *Ilustrirte vokh,* was announced on July 17, 1924 as follows:

> Veltshpigl *will encompass the whole world and will bring the Yiddish reader the most interesting accounts of people and places, of nations, their customs and lifestyles.*
>
> Veltshpigl *will cover the most sensational phenomena, happenings, discoveries, and in general, everything that occurs in the wide world and that almost never reaches readers of the daily papers.*
>
> Veltshpigl *will also strive in its geographic-ethnographic news to serve as a trusty guide for people who have a notion to visit certain places, to emigrate permanently, etc.*
>
> Veltshpigl *will be illustrated with original pictures of racial types, of various rare natural phenomena. In general, every account will be amply illustrated.*
>
> Veltshpigl *is prepared by the editors of* Ilustrirte vokh *and this alone provides the full assurance that it will be European in style and an exemplary publication in the Yiddish press.*

Indeed, the first issues contained illustrated essays about Australian aborigines, New Guinea headhunters, life in Bali and Tibet, the development of the airplane, and research on outer space, illustrated with a photograph of Mars taken in 1909.

In addition to these general magazines, there were illustrated periodicals that specialized in such subjects as theater and film—*Yidishe bine; Teater-velt; Filmtsaytung; Kin-te-rad: ilustrirte vokhnblat far kino, teater, un radio,* which was a popular magazine; and the more serious *Filmvelt,* which announced its aims in its first issue (1928) as follows:

> *Film, the new art form, has grown greatly in the last while, and has . . . infiltrated the lives of the largest folk masses in the whole world.*
>
> *In its triumphal move into every part of the world, film reaches the most isolated human community, and with its "naive muteness" unites the multilingual, many-colored nations, simultaneously eradicating the boundaries among race, nation, and class.*

We who pay tribute to this mute art are one family, tightly bound among ourselves by the love of and devotion to film.

In the sea of varied films, our periodical intends to be a leader and a guide for the Yiddish reader and filmgoer and desires to acquaint him with the various achievements and accomplishments in the international film domain, establishing at the same time a rigorous distinction between cheap sensationalism and true art. . . .

As indicated by these journals and the numerous reviews of films in other magazines, moving pictures attracted much interest in the press. In contrast, photography was almost never written about in the Jewish press—there was one very short-lived journal devoted to photography, *Der fotografist*—and the subject of Jewish photography in Poland still awaits full study.

Although Jewish newspapers in Poland never made extensive use of photography in their daily issues, some of them did put out weekly illustrated supplements—*Haynt*, *Der moment*, *Nasz Przegląd*, *Dziennik Warszawski*, *Chwila*. The first Yiddish daily to publish a weekly illustrated supplement was the *Jewish Daily Forward (Forverts)* in New York. The beautiful sepia roto-

Warsaw actors reading the Art Section of the *Jewish Daily Forward*, 1926. Photographer: Menakhem Kipnis/Raphael Abramovitch Collection

gravure "Art Section," as the supplement was called, was begun in 1923 and contained the first genuine photoessays and the best quality reproductions of photographs in the Yiddish press. At first, unrelated photographs on a general theme were grouped somewhat arbitrarily on the page; later, a photographer would cover an event—the wedding of the daughter of the *Bobover rebe*, the relief activities of ORT, the process of baking matzohs, the strike of the brushmakers in 1924, in Międzyrzec, a May 1 celebration—and the pictures would be arranged to tell a coherent story with no text except the captions.

In the Art Section, a page each was generally devoted to great paintings, current events, travel to faraway places, stars of stage and screen, the latest fashions, beauty contests, and "Picture contributions from our readers and correspondents." This last category dealt almost exclusively with traditional Jewish life in Eastern Europe—"Jewish trades in Vilna," "Three typical East European Jewish couples of the older generation," "Odd Jewish types in Europe," "Jewish poverty in Poland." Sensationalism, pathos, and humor emanated from these pages to engage the readers, many of whom were themselves often contributors. The captions were impressionistic— "Some shanty!—A ghetto street in Opatov, Poland"—and rhetorical—"Abraham Donde, a war victim for whom assistance is asked of Vilna and Kovno townsmen." Indeed, the page of Old World photographs published by the *Forward* was designed to assure immigrants newly arrived in the United States of the wisdom of their choice and to encourage them to assist the Jews who had remained in Eastern Europe.

In contrast, *Nasz Przegląd*, a Polish-language Zionist newspaper published in Warsaw, appealed to a cosmopolitan, somewhat assimilated middle-class Jewish reader living in urban centers. It emphasized modern Jewish cultural life in its Polish milieu. *Yidishe bilder*, which was published in Latvia, also presented modern Jewish life in photographs, but was more international both in coverage and distribution.

All of the illustrated Jewish papers discussed here

NASZ PRZEGLĄD
ILUSTROWANY

MISS JUDEA".

P. ZOFJA OLDAKÓWNA OTRZYMAŁA TYTUŁ „MISS JUDEA!" NA KONKURSIE PIĘK-
NOŚCI ZORGANIZOWANYM PRZEZ „NASZ PRZEGLĄD".
P. Oldakówna nosiła suknię ze srebrnej lamy i sortie gronostajowe z firmy M. Apfelbaum (Marszałkowska 125)

"Miss Judea." Zofja Oldak, winner of a beauty contest sponsored by *Nasz Przegląd*, the Warsaw Polish-Jewish newspaper, in 1929. "Miss Oldak is wearing a gown of silver lamé and an ermine wrap fashioned by M. Apfelbaum, 125 Marszałkowska Street." *Nasz Przegląd*, March 31, 1929

employed photographers active in Poland. The first photograph agency in Poland was established in 1910 by the journalist Marian Fuks, who became president of the Jewish Photographers' Guild in Warsaw. Such agencies provided the press with both local and international news photographs. But whereas the agency from which a photograph was obtained might be noted in the press, the photographers remained anonymous until the mid-twenties. In 1923, when the *Forward* featured "Contributions from our readers and correspondents," the photographers were identified for the first time, albeit as contributors to this particular page. On other pages, the *Forward* did not as a rule provide the photographers' names.

Most of the Yiddish illustrated magazines were international in subject matter, were distributed abroad, and obtained their photographs of Jewish life in Poland from a common cadre of photographers, the most prominent of whom were Menakhem Kipnis, Alter Kacyzne, Avrom Yosl Rotenberg,

1

2

3

4

Henryk Bojm, Moryc Grossman, L. Przedecki, and Wilhelm Aleksandrowitz. Although these men were professional, or in some cases, semiprofessional photographers, they were better known for other accomplishments.

Although the camera still remained a luxury, the number of amateur photographers increased dramatically after World War I, when Poland started producing more of her own photographic equipment. The earliest Polish amateur photography association, *Towarzystwo Miłośników Fotografii*, was

1 Alter Kacyzne (1885–1941), with his wife and daughter. Kacyzne was best known as a playwright, poet, and novelist, although he made his living from photography. Born in Vilna, he later moved to Warsaw, where he established a photography studio just after World War I. There he served the stars of the Yiddish stage and literary scene as well as the general trade. He was frequently asked to cover important political and social events, and his special interest in class conflict was expressed in his many photographs of strikes, the unemployed, and the poor. In 1921, HIAS (Hebrew Immigrant Aid Society) commissioned him to photograph all aspects of the emigration procedures conducted in their Warsaw offices and on the route to the harbor in Gdańsk (Danzig). During the thirties, Kacyzne was a major contributor of photographs to *Ilustrirte velt* and the rotogravure Art Section of the *Jewish Daily Forward*.

2 Menakhem Kipnis (1878–1942), *center*, with his wife and friends in Drohiczyn in the 1930s. Kipnis, who was born into a family of Hasidic rabbis and cantors in the Ukraine, was better known as a singer, folklore collector, and journalist than as a photographer. He easily combined these talents while wandering through Poland, taking photographs and writing his many articles on musical personages and events, folksongs he had recently collected, local characters, and Jewish folkways. Kipnis's photographs appeared in almost every major Jewish illustrated magazine in Yiddish and Polish, as did his articles. Photographer: I. Szwarc

3 Avrom Yosl Rotenberg, who had studied medicine and photography in Warsaw, worked as a paramedic in Staszów, the town of his birth, before turning his full attention to photography. The photographs that he and his family took of Jewish life in Staszów and its environs, especially of town characters and traditional scenes, were entered in various competitions and were published in many illustrated Jewish newspapers, most frequently in *Yidishe bilder* and the *Jewish Daily Forward*. Simkhe Rotenberg Collection

4 Tableau of a family, gathered around the holiday table. New Year's greeting card/Postcard: Verlag S. Resnik, Warsaw

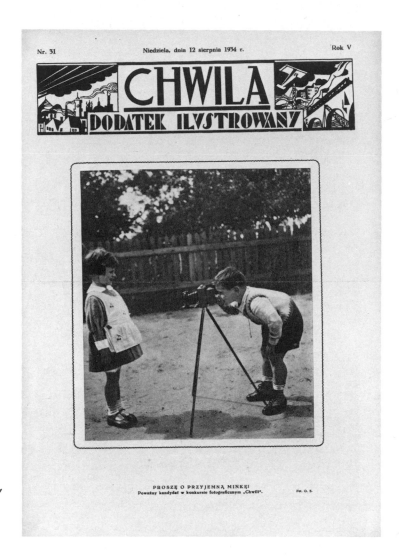

"'Say cheese.' A serious candidate
in the *Chwila* photographic contest."
Photographer: O.S. *Chwila: Dodatek
Ilustrowany*, August 12, 1934

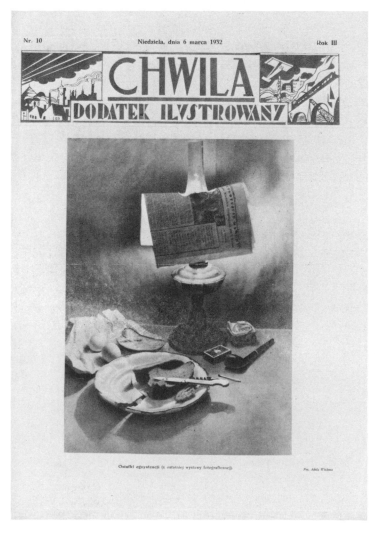

"The Remnants of Existence (from
the latest photographic exhibition)."
Photographer: Adela Wixlowa. *Chwila:
Dodatek Ilustrowany*, March 6, 1932

formed in 1891. Important for amateur Jewish photographers were such groups as the photographic section of the *Yidishe gezelshaft far landkentenish—Żydowske Towarzystwo Krajoznawcze* (Jewish Society for Hiking and Local History), which was founded in Warsaw in 1926 and had branches and an active following in most cities and towns in Poland. (Among the other sections and circles of this society were art, technology and industry, public health, ethnography, ecology, kayaking and skiing, music, and Esperanto.) A major aim of the Society was to support scholarly research on the history of Jewish settlement in Poland, especially as revealed through monuments, art, and folklore. Such distinguished scholars as N. Pryłucki, Emanuel Ringelblum, I. Schiper, R. Mahler, S. Zajczyk, and S. Lehman conducted courses, gave lectures, and organized exhibitions and excursions for various sections of the Society. Reports on the many activities undertaken appear in the Society's bilingual newsletter *Landkentenish—Krajoznawstwo*. The photographic section of the *Yidishe gezelshaft far landkentenish* stated its goals as follows:

> To photograph monuments of historic and artistic value and artifacts of folkloristic and ethnographic interest;
> To make a photographic record of excursions and to document Jewish organizational and social life as observed on these outings;
> To teach the theory and practice of photography and to further knowledge of Jewish photography;
> To maintain contact with historians and ethnographers and to seek their guidance;
> To raise the level of artistic photography and to free it from the influence of painting. *

Jewish journalists and archivists also undertook to gather photographs, whether original prints, postcards, or newspaper clippings. They understood the historical and news value of such material, and in several cases later published their collections, which often focused on a specific place or era, for example, Vilna and World War I. In terms of photographs,

*M. Dancygerkron, "Organizujemy koła i sekcje fotograficzne," *Krajoznawstwo* II, 2 (1936):8.

Gustav Eisner (1887–1939), a journalist who collected material pertaining to World War I. He emigrated to the United States in 1920.

Vilna is probably the best-documented Jewish community in Poland, thanks to the collecting and photographing efforts of Ephim Jeshurin, Moryc Grossman, Moshe Raviv, and recently, Lazar Ran. Jewish life in Poland during World War I was the subject of a collection made by Gustav Eisner, who at the time was city reporter for the *Lodzher togblat* and correspondent for *Haynt* in Warsaw.

The destruction of the Polish Jewish community during World War II totally transformed the way in which the photographs made before the war were perceived. As Raphael Abramovitch so poignantly stated, in retrospect, these photographs are "pictures taken by people who could not foresee that they were photographing, and thus immortalizing, a people on the eve of their destruction."*

Among the last pictures of this community are those taken by Roman Vishniac, the best-known photographer of East European Jewry, who traveled throughout Central and Eastern Europe between 1933 and 1939. His work was once described by Edward Steichen, compiler of *The Family of Man*, as being "among photography's finest documents of a time and place."†

*Raphael Abramovitch, *The Vanished World* (New York: Forward Association, 1947), p. 11.
†Roman Vishniac, *Roman Vishniac*. International Center for Photography Library of Photographers, vol. 6 (New York: Grossman Publishers, 1974), p. [5].

Vishniac's photographs were first exhibited in the United States at the YIVO Institute for Jewish Research in 1944. Thirty of them were published by Schocken Books three years later in the volume *Polish Jews*, which has remained in print for thirty years. Today, Roman Vishniac lives in New York City, where he teaches photography and continues his lifelong work in photomicroscopy.

In 1947, the same year that Vishniac's *Polish Jews* appeared, Raphael Abramovitch published *The Vanished World*. In the introduction he wrote:

> *Vanished are the Jewish quarters in Polish, Rumanian and Galician cities, even if the cities themselves managed to escape the holocaust. Where previously millions led a tumultuous life, desolate thousands now roam in misery. No more the markets, the bustling Jewish business sections, the Yeshivas, the Talmud academies, the workers' open-air centers with their meetings and fervid discussions, the Jewish newspapers with hundreds of thousands of readers, the teeming community mass life—no longer do they exist and never again in this setting can they be resurrected. Our Old World is a Vanished World. . . .**

This comprehensive commemorative portrait of East European Jewry consists of 530 photographs drawn from the 1944 exhibition of Roman Vishniac and from the enormous archives of original prints that the *Forward* had received from its correspondents in Poland—Alter Kacyzne; Menakhem Kipnis, Avrom Yosl Rotenberg, and others.

The contrast between prewar and postwar treatments of Polish Jewry in compilations of photographs is particularly dramatic in the two collections published by Moshe Raviv (Vorobeichic), a painter living in Israel today. He took photographs during the 1920s and 1930s, and in 1931 sixty-five of his "photo-compositions," or photomontages, appeared in a book entitled *The Ghetto Lane of Vilna*, published in Zurich by Orell Fussli in a Hebrew-English edition and in a Hebrew-German edition. This volume is a rare example of avant-garde Jewish art photography and shows the influence of Man Ray

*Abramovitch, p. 10.

Photomontage by M. Vorobeichic (Moshe Raviv) titled "Awaiting Customers." From M. Vorobeichic, *The Ghetto Lane in Vilna: 65 Pictures* (Zurich and Leipzig: Orell Fussli Publishers, 1931), plate 36.

and Moholy-Nagy. (Raviv had studied art at Vilna University, the Bauhaus, and the Academie des Beaux Arts in Paris, and Fernand Léger had written a preface for Raviv's volume of photomontages of Paris published the same year as the Vilna volume.) In 1946 in Palestine, Raviv selected ten of his documentary photographs for a portfolio which he entitled *Poland* and which he offered as an epitaph to a destroyed community.

The vanished world has been the dominating theme of almost all subsequent pictorial presentations of Polish Jewry. Perhaps the most important of these are the hundreds of richly illustrated memorial volumes that commemorate specific Jewish communities in Poland and that have been issued by the survivors. The finest photographic album of a Polish Jewish community, published by Lazar Ran in 1974, is devoted to Vilna and is entitled *Jerusalem of Lithuania*. In recent years, several comprehensive compilations have appeared—Michał Borwicz's *A Thousand Years of Jewish Life in Poland*, Abraham Shulman's *The Old Country: The Lost World of East European Jewry*, and Franz Hubman's *The Jewish Family Album: The Life of a People in Photographs*.

Such volumes were made possible through the efforts of the many organizations and individuals who took and collected photographs. One of the most important of these institutions is the YIVO Institute for Jewish Research, which from its inception in Vilna in 1925, gathered, preserved, catalogued, exhibited, and published photographs and other materials concerning all aspects of Jewish life. In 1940, the YIVO headquarters were transferred to New York. The Germans, who occupied Vilna in 1941, confiscated the YIVO archives. Avrom Sutzkever and Shmerke Kaczerginsky, Yiddish writers and YIVO associates, were forced by the Nazis to inventory the confiscated archives and library. Risking their lives, they managed to hide and later retrieve some of the materials. Most of the archives and library were destroyed, however. The rest was transported to Frankfurt by the Nazis, and a part of it was recovered after the war through the efforts of the United States Department of State and American military authorities in Germany. The rescued material was eventually returned to the YIVO in New York.

The photographs from the recovered archives today form the most valuable part of YIVO's pictorial holdings. Especially rich in the area of East European Jewish culture before World War II, the YIVO's collection of 100,000 photographs also covers other parts of the world, the Holocaust, and Jewish life in America, especially during the period of mass settlement. The Polish collection alone consists of some 10,000 photographs, not counting the pictures made in Poland that are in the theater collection and in the files on famous people. In addition, the YIVO possesses the finest collection of Jewish periodicals published in Poland, including most of the illustrated magazines and supplements.

During the postwar years this collection has greatly expanded, mainly as a result of donations from individuals and organizations. The most notable recent contributions include the extraordinary photographs that Roman Vishniac made just before the outbreak of World War II and donated to YIVO in 1944; several beautiful prints by Moshe Raviv; the photographs Raphael Abramovitch gathered for his book *The Vanished World*; the Gustav Eisner collection of postcards and photographs from the World War I period; photographs from Kazimierz nad Wisłą, made by Jerzy Dorys in the 1930s; original prints from the archives of two important American Yiddish dailies, the *Forward* and *Der tog*; materials from the Jewish Labor Bund Archives in New York; and the albums and photographs of various Jewish-American relief, educational, and immigrant-aid organizations, including the American Joint Distribution Committee, HIAS, and ORT.

The American Joint Distribution Committee sent representatives to Poland after World War I to aid the Jewish community; while there they documented the ravages of war and their own efforts at reconstruction. They made many albums of views of towns and cities, and photographic reports on sanitary conditions, especially public bathhouses and *mikves* (ritual baths), orphanages, homes for the aged, health care, and other subjects. One of the most valuable parts of the collection deposited at YIVO by HIAS is the series of more than a hundred photographs taken by Alter Kacyzne of the emigration process in HIAS's Warsaw offices.

The family of the late Salman and Theodore Schocken recently donated to YIVO a very important collection of sixty-seven glass negatives of twelve wooden synagogues in various parts of northeastern Poland. The negatives, which most probably were made just before and during World War I, were gathered together in preparation for the *Encyclopaedia Judaica: Das Judentum in Geschichte und Gegenwart*, the first volume of which was published in 1928. In 1934, shortly after the Nazi

From a photographer's family album.
Self-portrait of L. Karp with his daughter.
Skierniewice, 1921

takeover in Germany, the project was interrupted at the letter "L" and the last volumes were never published. Some of the glass negatives were used in the first ten volumes.

In 1944, after settling in its new headquarters in New York, YIVO undertook a project, "Museum of the Homes of the Past," the aim of which was "the collection and preservation of all the materials that reflect the history, the life, the communal and individual problems of Jews in Eastern Europe and of their contributions to the culture and organization of society during the past eighty to one hundred years."* An important part of the resulting collection was photographs gathered from East European Jews living in America.

Knowing that the fate of family photographs is a precarious one, many people deposited with and continue to donate to YIVO their family albums, snapshots, postcards and memora-

*Yedies fun YIVO—Newsletter of the YIVO 3 (July 1944): 2.

bilia, and home movies. This material is of extraordinary value, especially in light of the fact that most of the photographic records of Polish Jewish life suffered the same fate as their subjects. Indeed, many Jews who passed as Gentiles in order to survive, were forced to destroy their family pictures, which might otherwise serve as evidence against them.

Today, the YIVO Institute for Jewish Research continues in New York City the work it began in Vilna. The collections it has assembled and the research it has sponsored form the basis for this volume.

Part Two
The Persistence of the Past

SETTLEMENTS

Even before the establishment of the first Polish kingdom in the tenth century, Jewish merchants visited Poland in the course of their journeys. While the very first settlers came from the east in the tenth century, the earliest large-scale migrations to Poland, between the twelfth and fifteenth centuries, were from the west. Most of the settlers fled from German lands and Bohemia during the Crusades and the period of the Black Death. They were followed by Jews who sought asylum in Poland and other countries after their expulsion from Spain and Portugal in 1492–1493.

Unlike the largely peasant Slavic populations, the Jews were city dwellers and skilled craftsmen. They also were experienced in trade and fiscal matters. Polish kings and princes, who welcomed the contribution the Jews could make to Poland's economic development, encouraged them to settle and offered them protection.

With the unification of Poland and Lithuania in 1569, the newly-formed Commonwealth extended from the Baltic to the Black Sea, and included within its boundaries Poles, Ukrainians, White Russians, Lithuanians, and others. Jews, who had taken part in the early development of towns and cities in Poland proper, now played a major role in the colonization of the outlying areas of the Commonwealth. Active in local commerce, they also exercised a virtual monopoly over entire branches of national and international trade, for example, timber and hides. Many were employed as tax collectors and as stewards of estates and industries belonging to the nobility, including salt mines, mills, and the production and sale of alcoholic beverages.

During the fifteenth and sixteenth centuries, the Golden Age of Polish Jewry, the Jews enjoyed relative freedom within the feudal structure of Poland. They could travel inside and outside the country, engage in a variety of occupations, and

Wysock, a tiny village in Volhynia,
1937. Photographer: Moshe Raviv

A gentile wet nurse
holding a Jewish child.
Równe, 1921.
Dr. Jacob J. Golub
Collection

A well in a rural area in Volhynia, not far from the Polish-Russian border.

Mountain Jews in
Rosochacz, a village
in the Eastern Beskid
range of the Car-
pathian mountains.
Der tog Collection

Jews and peasants in a
village in the Carpathian
mountains, 1921.

An elderly wanderer and his grandson en route between Warsaw and Otwock, one of the many rural towns that surround the capital, 1928. Photographer: Menakhem Kipnis

practice their religion and self-government. These rights, which were basic to their way of life, depended on privileges granted to them by the generally sympathetic kings and nobility. However, pressures from the townspeople, their economic competitors, and from the clergy, who objected to their faith, forced even tolerant rulers to place restrictions on the place and manner in which Jews might live. Individual cities were at times granted the privilege *de non tolerandis Judaeis*, which meant that Jews could not live within their limits. Sometimes Jews were compelled to live within designated areas within the towns. They were also banned from various spheres of economic and social life.

Wooden foot bridge in Maciejowice, one of the oldest Jewish settlements in Lublin province. Photographer: Alter Kacyzne/Raphael Abramovitch Collection

The store and home of Yankev and Perl Rebejkow on a street in Jeziory, ca. 1900. The sign in Russian advertises their wares—grain, flour, groats, and bran.

1 Zabłudów, 1916. A town famous for its seventeenth-century wooden synagogue.

2 Market day in Hrubieszów, 1925. Photographer: Alter Kacyzne/Raphael Abramovitch Collection

3 Water pump in the fish market in Otwock, twenty-eight kilometers southeast of Warsaw. Photographer: Alter Kacyzne/Raphael Abramovitch Collection

Jews were resourceful in coping with such restrictions. When they were excluded from city markets, they engaged in foreign trade. If they were forbidden to live in cities, they settled in nearby towns. Most important, their communities developed a form of self-governing, administrative organization, the kehillah. Institutionally complete and autonomous, the Jewish community had its own schools, hospitals, courts of law, and welfare organizations. From ca. 1580 to 1764, local Jewish communities were subject to the Council of the Four Lands, the supreme authority regulating the communal life of Polish Jewry.

2

3

The seventeenth and eighteenth centuries saw the end of the Golden Age of Polish Jewry. The country was weakened by war and internal conflict. In the years 1772–1795, Poland was partitioned and absorbed by neighboring Austria, Prussia, and Russia, who were to dominate her for almost one hundred and fifty years. The Jews, like the rest of the population, were divided among these three countries, in which they confronted economic, political, and cultural conditions very different from those they had known before the partitions. Even though during the nineteenth and twentieth centuries radical changes—increasing secularization, development of modern industry, emancipation—took place, basic patterns of Jewish settlement, communal organization, and occupation persisted up until the eve of World War II.

Cracow

One of Poland's oldest cities and once its capital, Cracow was a medieval center of commerce and manufacture in southwestern Poland. Famous for its art, it was also the site of one of the earliest universities in Europe (founded 1364), where Nicholas Copernicus once studied.

Although Jewish merchants in the tenth century followed the trade routes that intersected in Cracow, Jewish settlement there began in the twelfth or thirteenth century. In 1494, as a result of conflicts with the Christian townspeople and clergy, the Jews were expelled to the suburb of Kazimierz, which became an exclusively Jewish town (*Communitas Judaeorum Casimirensium Ad Cracoviam*). Even though their residence was restricted to Kazimierz, they were permitted to enter Cracow to conduct their affairs.

In the four centuries preceding the final partition of Poland in 1795, Cracow played a vital role in Jewish commercial and intellectual life in Eastern Europe. It was the home of celebrated physicians and rabbinical scholars, the most notable of whom were Jacob Pollack and Moses Isserles.

Entrance to the Jewish quarter in Cracow, 1938. Photographer: Roman Vishniac

Aerial view of Cracow. Raphael Abramovitch Collection

Warsaw

Between the tenth and thirteenth centuries, Warsaw grew from a hamlet to an urban center. In 1596 the official capital of Poland was moved there from Cracow by the Polish king Sigismund III Vasa.

After a short period of Jewish settlement in the city, Warsaw was granted the privilege *de non tolerandis Judaeis* in 1527. Expelled from Warsaw, Jews settled on its outskirts in the so-called *jurydykas* (private estates) of Polish noble families. As in Cracow, the Jews were allowed to enter Warsaw for specified purposes; during sessions of the Polish Parliament they came into the city to sell merchandise, to act as advisors to the Polish nobles, and to intercede on behalf of the Jewish population. With the expansion of the city, the *jurydykas* were incorporated into the metropolis. The Jews of Warsaw eventually became the single largest Jewish community in Europe.

In the final partition of Poland in 1795, Warsaw was given to Prussia. From 1807 until 1813, Warsaw was the capital of the Grand Duchy of Warsaw. Following the defeat of Napoleon, in 1815, it fell under Russian domination, where it remained until the Germans occupied it during World War I. After 1918, Warsaw became the capital of the Second Polish Republic.

Rynek Starego Miasta (Old City Market), inside the medieval walls of Warsaw, 1938. Photographer: Roman Vishniac

Vilna

Vilna, once the capital of the Grand Duchy of Lithuania, is situated in northeastern Poland. The architectural magnificence of the city reflects Vilna's importance in the economic and intellectual life of the Commonwealth of Poland and Lithuania (1569–1795) and, later, as a stronghold of the Reformation in Poland and the birthplace of Polish Romanticism.

Jews began to settle in Vilna in the fifteenth century. The Jewish community developed after the union of Poland and Lithuania in the sixteenth century. It occupied one whole street in the middle of the town and built its first synagogue toward the end of the sixteenth century. Eventually, there were almost one hundred synagogues and prayer houses in Vilna.

Though modest in size, Vilna was called the "Jerusalem of Lithuania." A center of Jewish religious thought, it was the city of the renowned Rabbi Elijah (the Gaon of Vilna) and the home of many other great Talmudic scholars. In the nineteenth century, in northeastern Poland, the Jewish Enlightenment first took root in Vilna. The city was also a major center of Hebrew and Yiddish cultural and national movements.

Panorama of Vilna on the Wilia River. Ephim H. Jeshurin Collection

Jatkowa (Meatmarket) Street in the old Jewish quarter of Vilna. Ephim H. Jeshurin Collection/Postcard: W. Borkowski, Vilna

Three Other Cities

The Jewish quarter in the old section of Lublin, 1938. Photographer: Roman Vishniac

Market day in Krzemieniec, 1925. One of the oldest settlements in eastern Poland.
Photographer: Alter Kacyzne

Sale of clothing at the market in Kazimierz nad Wisłą (Yiddish: *Kuzmir*), ca. 1920.
Photographer: Alter Kacyzne

"THE KNOT OF LIFE"

Ancient cemeteries and their ornate tombstones provide evidence of the earliest settlement of Jews on Polish soil. The oldest Jewish tombstone yet discovered is that of David ben Shalom, a Polish Jew who died in Wrocław (Breslau) on the twenty-fifth day of Av 4963 (1203). One of the oldest known Jewish cemeteries in Poland was in Kalisz and dates from 1287.

An organized Jewish community by definition had its own kehillah (communal self-government), and a house of prayer,

Jews praying at the tombstone of REMA (Rabbi Moses Isserles) on Lag ba'Omer, the anniversary of his death. REMA, who died in 1572, is buried near the synagogue in Cracow that bears his name. Photographer: Menakhem Kipnis/ Raphael Abramovitch Collection

1

2

3

4   5

1   The tomb of Rabbi Elijah (1720–1797), the Vilna Gaon. Behind the tomb can be seen the tree which sprang, according to legend, from the graveside of Walentyn Potocki, Polish nobleman and convert to Judaism. Photographer: Moryc Grossman/Raphael Abramovitch Collection

2   Tombstone of Jacob Meshullam ben Mordecai Ze'ev Ornstein (1775–1839), the great Talmudist, in the old cemetery in Lwów. The relief on the tombstone shows the four volumes of his famous work, the *Yeshu'ot Ya'akov,* a commentary on the Shulhan Arukh. Photographer: Antonina Marbach

3   Tombstones in the old Jewish cemetery in Stryj. The 18th-century tombstone in the foreground is decorated with a relief of the Polish eagle. Photographer: Dr. Schnir

4   Family gathered at a tombstone in the cemetery in Włoszczowa. The tombstone bears the inscription: "A righteous man who led a life of good deeds, who lived from the fruits of his labor all his years, who died young, who was a giver of charity, the worthy one, Yisroel Yitskhok, son of Shmuel Zindl, may his memory be blessed . . . May his soul be tied in the knot of life." Studio: A. Pieczysty

5   Professional mourners *(klogerins)* in the cemetery in Brody. During the month of Elul, it was customary to visit the graves of relatives and of very pious Jews to pray for eternal rest for the deceased and to beg them to intervene with God on behalf of the living. Professional mourners were sometimes hired to improvise prayers and entreaties in Yiddish; they wailed and fell upon the graves, in a show of mourning. Herbert Achtentuch Collection

mikve (ritual bath), and cemetery. In medieval Poland, Jewish settlements that lacked one or another of these institutions had to utilize the facilities of neighboring communities. Some settlements, outgrowths of earlier established communities, were denied cemeteries or other institutions of their own by the older kehillahs in order to keep them dependent on the parent communities. Thus Żółkiew remained under the jurisdiction of the Lwów kehillah, and Sambor under the Przemyśl kehillah.

The right of other Jewish settlements to establish cemeteries was sometimes denied by the church or the local Christian municipality. Jewish cemeteries were also not permitted in cities that had been granted the privilege *de non tolerandis Judaeis*, although these often had some Jewish inhabitants. Thus the Jews who were allowed to remain in Warsaw after the official expulsion in 1527 had to bury their dead in nearby Sochaczew and Grodzisk.

Tombstones, in themselves a source of information on genealogy and settlement history, are also valuable for the study of Jewish iconography and art. They vary from simple slab forms to imposing sarcophagus-like tombs. Their florid relief carvings were often painted in bright colors and varnished to protect them from the elements.

SYNAGOGUES

Although every Jewish community was expected to devote a space to communal prayer, a building constructed for this purpose alone was not required. Nonetheless, synagogues were built even in the smallest towns. Jewish guilds and members of different occupations often established their own prayer houses, as did Hasidic courts, whose *shtiblekh* or *kloyzn* were arranged to accommodate Hasidic styles of meeting and prayer. In rare cases, for example, in Brześć nad Bugiem (Yiddish: *Brisk*), there was also a special synagogue for women.

The synagogue fulfilled the functions both of communal prayer and of public assembly. For example, the Great City Synagogue of Vilna, in the heart of the medieval Jewish quarter, was begun in 1630 and developed into a complex of fourteen structures around a courtyard. It included prayer halls, kehillah building, *mikve* (ritual bath), rabbinical library, and individual *kloyzn* (small synagogues) for various guilds,

Interior of the Old Synagogue of Kazimierz (Cracow). Built in the late fourteenth century, it is the oldest remaining synagogue in Poland. From Majer Bałaban, *Historja Żydów w Krakowie i na Kazimierzu 1304–1868,* vol. 1 (Cracow: Nadzieja, 1931)

Kune (pillory), attached to the wall of the anteroom of the seventeenth-century synagogue in Przysucha. In parts of medieval Poland, the kehillah, acting as a court of law, sometimes sentenced an offender to be pilloried. The *kune* was locked around the prisoner's neck, hands, or feet. Photographer: L. Przedecki

The great fortress synagogue of Łuck, built during the seventeenth century on the site of an older wooden synagogue. It was constructed in the form of a fortress to help defend the city against the invasions of the Cossacks and Tatars. Photographer: Menakhem Kipnis/*Forward* Collection

The synagogue in Orla. Originally a Calvinist church, the building was sold to the Jews of Orla in 1732, after the failure of the Calvinist movement in Poland. Salman Schocken Collection

The Tłomackie Synagogue in Warsaw. Built between 1872 and 1878, and designed by Leandro Marconi, an Italian architect, it was destroyed by the Germans during the Warsaw Ghetto uprising. The Royal Library of Copenhagen Collection

The synagogue in the Free City of Gdańsk (Danzig), built in 1881 and destroyed by the Germans in 1940. In 1939 the Jewish community in Gdańsk, realizing that war was imminent, sent the treasured objects from the Gdańsk Synagogue to The Jewish Theological Seminary in New York for safekeeping. Today these objects are at The Jewish Museum in New York.

Worshipers leaving the Altshtot (Old City) Synagogue on Wolborska Street, Łódź, 1937. On November 11, 1939, the twenty-first anniversary of Poland's independence, this and three other great synagogues and the Kościuszko monument in Łódź were destroyed by the Germans. Photographer: Moshe Raviv

societies, and Hasidic courts. The oldest synagogues in Poland are believed to have stood in Kalisz (1264) and Płock (1237). The form of Polish masonry synagogues, the oldest type known to us, was influenced by many foreign styles—Gothic, Byzantine, Italian Renaissance, Baroque—as was customary in Polish architecture of the time.

The earliest pictorial records of wooden synagogues show none built earlier than the mid-seventeenth century, but it can be assumed that they existed well before this time. There are indications that masonry synagogues built in the sixteenth century replaced earlier wooden structures destroyed by fire or war. Also, the long tradition of Polish vernacular timber architecture, which is the basis for the wooden synagogues, predates masonry synagogues. The wooden synagogues were in the main modeled on local town halls, granaries or barns, manor houses, and churches.

Exterior of the famed eighteenth-century wooden synagogue in Wołpa. The interior is elaborately carved and decorated. Salman Schocken Collection

Interior of the magnificent seventeenth-century wooden synagogue in Zabłudów, showing the *bime*, the raised podium from which the Torah is read and, on Rosh Hashanah, the shofar sounded. Salman Schocken Collection

Exterior of the eighteenth-century wooden synagogue in Jeziory. Salman Schocken Collection

Wooden synagogues were commonly built in the small towns of Great Poland, Galicia, Volhynia, and the Lithuanian part of the Commonwealth. Whereas the Galician examples were famous for their elaborately decorated interiors, especially their wall paintings, those in the northeast were known for their fine woodwork and paneling. The wooden synagogues are testimony to the intimate and creative aspects of Polish-Jewish interaction. Jewish carpenters created a synthesis in which Polish construction techniques, materials, and architectural forms interacted with the requirements of Jewish religious observance and its symbolism.

Szymon Zajczyk

Szymon Zajczyk was one of the foremost specialists in the history of synagogues and Jewish sculpture in Poland. He was a student and protégé of Oskar Sosnowski, Majer Bałaban, and Stanisław Herbst, eminent Polish and Jewish historians and historians of architecture. The Warsaw Polytechnic and the Polish Ministry of Religion and Education sponsored Zajczyk's expeditions into various regions of Poland, where he investigated Jewish synagogues, cemeteries, and artifacts. Unable to support his family, Zajczyk also worked as a photographer and documented Jewish material culture by means of thousands of excellent photographs.

His major achievements include publications on the wooden synagogues in the Białystok region (1929), the Baroque masonry synagogues in Poland (1933), and the synagogues in Zamość and Kępno. Some of his studies were posthumously published by Polish friends after World War II. His architectural drawings and photographs have served as the basic source for subsequent scholarly works on synagogues, one of the most well known being Maria and Kazimierz Piechotka's *Wooden Synagogues* (Warsaw, 1957).

During the German occupation, in 1940, Zajczyk and his family were confined in the Warsaw ghetto. With the help of his former professor, Stanisław Herbst, they later escaped to the "Aryan side," where, in hiding, Zajczyk continued to write. On June 4, 1943, he was discovered and killed.

Religious Functionaries

The *klekoydesh* were officials paid by the kehillah to carry out functions vital to religious and communal life. Not all communities could afford to support the full range of offices, among which were the offices of rabbi, cantor, sexton *(shames)*, ritual slaughterer, scribe, bath attendant, cemetery watchman, resident preacher, and Talmud Torah teacher.

1

1 Moyshe Pinczuch, a *shames* (sexton) for forty years. Wysokie Litewskie, 1924. The *shames* served many functions. His main function was to care for the synagogue. He might also serve as leader of prayer, charity collector, notary, clerk, or bailiff. Photographer: Alter Kacyzne/ Raphael Abramovitch Collection

2 Yisrolik Szyldewer, a Hasid and *baldarshn* (preacher), in Staszów. Photographer: Avrom Yosl Rotenberg family/*Forward* Art Section, May 20, 1923

3 Dovid Elye, the *soyfer* (scribe). Annopol, ca. 1912. The *soyfer* prepared Torah scrolls, phylacteries, mezuzoth, amulets, and wedding certificates. Abraham Rechtman Collection

2

3

HASIDISM

For Polish Jewry the seventeenth and eighteenth centuries were catastrophic. In a single decade, 1648–1658, as a result of the Cossack uprisings led by Chmielnicki, an estimated seven hundred Jewish communities were destroyed and their inhabitants uprooted. During the century that followed, Poland was invaded by the Swedes, Turks, and Russians. Wars and internal dissension led to Poland's downfall at the end of the eighteenth century. Jewish communal life was undermined; its local kehillahs were enfeebled and, in 1764, its supreme body, the Council of the Four Lands was dissolved.

Confronted with these disasters, Jews, especially those in southeastern areas bordering on the Ottoman empire, embraced short-lived messianic movements led by leaders such as Shabbetai Zevi. Only Hasidism, which also originated as a small sect in this area, grew into a mass revivalist movement and a way of life within the Jewish community.

Palace of the *Tshortkever rebe* Moshe David Friedman (d. 1903) of the Sadogora Hasidic dynasty, in Czortków. Postcard

1

2

The wedding of the daughter of the *Bobover rebe* Ben-Zion Halberstam of Bobowa. Photographer: Wilhelm Aleksandrowitz/*Forward* Art Section, April 19, 1931

1 Two Hasidim masquerading as Polish officers of an earlier time entertain the wedding party with feats of swordsmanship.
2 The "commander-in-chief" of the *rebe*'s own guards, dressed in military uniform, leads the parade to greet the groom on his arrival.
3 The "Maharajah of *Bobov*," a Hasid on guard at the entrance to the Court.

3

The *Gerer rebe* Abraham Mordecai Alter
(d. 1948), the great-grandson of the
founder of one of the most famous and
powerful Hasidic dynasties in Poland.

Hasidim outside a house of prayer on Saturday. Cracow, 1938. Photographer: Roman Vishniac

Hasidim and others at Krynica-Zdrój, the most famous spa in Poland, in the 1930s.
Photographer: Menakhem Kipnis/Raphael Abramovitch Collection

Galician Jew. Postcard: Artysty, Stanisławów, 1904

Sholem David Unger
(d. 1923), the *Zhabner
rebe,* of Żabno.

Hasidism was founded by Israel ben Eliezer Ba'al Shem Tov (d. 1760) in Podolia and Volhynia. The movement spread from its original home in southeastern Poland to take root in Galicia, White Russia, Lithuania, and Congress Poland. At first Hasidism encountered severe opposition, especially in Vilna, from the rabbinate, who violently objected to its departures from rabbinic Judaism—its emphasis upon piety over Talmudic learning, its slight revisions of the prayer book and service, its mystical and Kabbalistic leanings, and the other ways in which it distinguished itself from and challenged the religious establishment.

Hasidism's broad appeal stemmed from its tenet that the humblest believer was as worthy as the most erudite Talmudist and that devotion to God could best be expressed through passionate prayer. In the course of time, study of the Talmud came to be accepted as necessary preparation for proper observance and prayer. The style of leadership was charismatic and, in time, dynastic: a *tsadik* or *rebe* led a local center or court and usually was succeeded by his son.

By the first half of the nineteenth century Hasidism had reached its highest point—a majority of the Orthodox Jews in Poland had joined the movement and it was accepted by the religious establishment. Powerful dynastic courts had developed in the Polish towns of Lublin, Kock, *Ger*, Aleksandrów, and Bełz. With the growth of secularism and of modern social and political movements in the late nineteenth century, the influence of Hasidism declined. The Hasidic movement continued nevertheless to maintain its special character and to provide a total and distinctive way of life for its adherents.

A LIFE OF STUDY...

In preparation for a life of piety and study, boys were sent to *kheyder*, a traditional primary school usually conducted in the home of a *melamed* (*kheyder* teacher). They sometimes entered

Kheyder boy. Warsaw, 1938. Photographer: Roman Vishniac

Yitskhok Erlich, the *belfer* (helper of the *melamed*), carries youngsters to *kheyder* in Staszów. The *belfer* was responsible for bringing the children to school and for keeping order once they were there. Photographer: Avrom Yosl Rotenberg family/Simkhe Rotenberg Collection

kheyder at the age of three. At four or five they had begun to learn the alphabet and the order of the prayers. In the second stage of their studies they read portions of the Pentateuch, and in the third phase they began to study the Talmud. To ensure that all males in the community received a religious education, the kehillah subsidized special public schools (Talmud Torahs) for the poor or paid their tuition at a private *kheyder*.

At twelve or thirteen, boys who did well in their studies could enter the yeshivah. Their studies there concluded with ordination at the age of nineteen or twenty. The yeshivahs

Boys' *kheyder*. Lublin, 1924. The *melamed* uses a special pointer to teach the Hebrew alphabet. Photographer: Alter Kacyzne/Raphael Abramovitch Collection

Girls' *kheyder* in Łaskarzew. Photographer: Alter Kacyzne/Raphael Abramovitch Collection

Yeshivah students on Nalewki Street. Warsaw, 1928. Photographer: Menakhem Kipnis/Raphael Abramovitch Collection

were generally supported by kehillahs and religious organizations, who also helped needy students. Poorer students from other towns were provided with meals by the local townspeople. Sometimes an older, married student was assisted by his father-in-law, who, as part of the bridal dowry, contracted to support the youth and his wife for a period of time.

Formal education ended for many young men when they had to seek work, sometimes even before they had completed *kheyder*. However, they often continued to study informally in

Men studying the Talmud in the *besmedresh* of a home for the aged at 17 Portowa Street, Vilna, 1937. Photographer: Moryc Grossman/ Raphael Abramovitch Collection

Women's executive board of the Orla Talmud Torah, 1930s. A. J. Smith Collection

the *besmedresh* (house of study). There men of all ages came daily to study alone or in small groups. There were also associations devoted to the study of various parts of the sacred literature.

Girls who received a religious education attended a girls' *kheyder* or were taught at home by a private tutor. Girls began learning to read Hebrew and Yiddish at the age of seven or eight. They read sacred texts like the *Tsene-rene*—the Pentateuch in a traditional Yiddish version intended for female readers. Their formal education usually stopped at the age of thirteen or fourteen.

During the nineteenth and early twentieth centuries, Jews were admitted to public schools, including universities, and Jewish secular school systems developed. Nonetheless, traditional patterns of study persisted in which the *kheyder* and yeshivah continued to play a major role. Even these institutions underwent modernization, and some introduced secular subjects into their curriculum. In addition, religious schools that provided formal education for girls were established.

CELEBRATION...

For every day, week, month, and year in the lifetime of the Jew there is a cycle of religious observance. Indeed, about one out of every four days of the Jewish year is a holy day of some kind, whether Sabbath, festival, or fast day.

The Sabbath is the high point of the weekly cycle. Women play a special role in ritual observances in the home and in the elaborate preparations that are made to ensure that the Sabbath is a day of rest and joy. A Jew must observe six hundred and thirteen religious commandments; women pay special attention to three—the burning of a piece of hallah dough when hallah is baked (symbolizing the giving of tithes to the priest); the lighting of candles to signal the onset of the Sabbath; and observance of the laws of family purity.

The annual round of festivals, fasts, and minor holidays is associated with the biblical seasons and with critical events in Jewish history. The ancient seasonal festivals of Passover, Shavuot, and Sukkot are mentioned in the Pentateuch in con-

"Very good and beautiful hallahs for the Sabbath. Egg hallahs also." Cracow, 1938. Photographer: Roman Vishniac/Raphael Abramovitch Collection

Housewives in Białystok carry *tsholnt,* a dish of meat, potatoes, and beans, to the baker's oven on Friday afternoon. The heat retained by the oven walls at the end of the day slowly cooked the *tsholnt* and kept it hot for the main meal on Saturday, when cooking was prohibited. *Forward* Art Section, November 20, 1932

Ezrielke the *shames* (sexton) was also the *shabes-klaper*. Biała, 1926. He knocked on shutters to let people know that the Sabbath was about to begin. Photographer: Alter Kacyzne/Raphael Abramovitch Collection

The interior of the old *mikve* (ritual bath) in Zaleszczyki. Men and women bathed at the *mikve,* especially before the Sabbath and other holidays. Ritual immersion was required of women after menstruation.

Blessing the candles. New Year's greeting card. Postcard: Verlag Jehudia, Warsaw

Returning from the synagogue. Chodorów, 1938. Photographer: Roman Vishniac

Reading the *Tsene-rene,* a Yiddish version of the Pentateuch. Vilna.

nection with the story of the Exodus from Egypt. Biblical and postbiblical events in which Jews were also saved from disaster are celebrated on such "minor" holidays as Hanukkah, Purim, and Lag ba'Omer. The catastrophe of the destruction of the Temple is solemnly commemorated on four separate fast days. Each year begins with the Days of Awe, a time of spiritual regeneration.

In addition to observances that are part of a calendric cycle there are those rituals that mark transitions in the lifetime of the individual—circumcision and redemption of the firstborn, Bar Mitzvah, betrothal and marriage, death. Indeed each day of the individual's life, even his most humble act, is accompanied by ritual and prayer.

1 Reform Jew wishes a Hasid a happy New Year. New Year's greeting card. Postcard: Verlag Jehudia, Warsaw

2 *Tashlikh*—"And thou wilt cast all their sins into the depth of the sea." Micah 7:19. On Rosh Hashanah, Jews pray at a stream and, according to custom, empty the contents of their pockets into the water, symbolically casting away their sins. New Year's greeting card. Verlag Jehudia, Warsaw

3 *Shlogn kapores*—a rite performed on the day before Yom Kippur. A person's sins are symbolically transferred to a fowl, which is sacrificed on his behalf. New Year's greeting card. Postcard: Verlag Jehudia, Warsaw

"As many *sukkot* as there are families." Cracow, 1937. On Sukkot, Jews eat, sleep, and study in temporary dwellings like those in which their ancestors lived in the wilderness after the Exodus from Egypt.

Examining the etrog (citron) for imperfections. The etrog is one of the "four species" of plants blessed on Sukkot. Studio: Kuszer, Warsaw

Buying flags for children to carry in the Torah procession on the eve of Simhat Torah, the last day of Sukkot, when the year-long reading of the Torah scroll is concluded. Studio: Kuszer, Warsaw

Khanike-gelt—coins are given to children on Hanukkah, a holiday celebrating the victory of the Maccabees. New Year's greeting card. Postcard: Verlag Jehudia, Warsaw

Purim-shpiler in Szydłowiec, 1937. *Purim-shpiler* performed traditional plays on Purim, a Jewish holiday celebrating the deliverance of the Jews from Haman's plot.

לכבוד פסח...—„צי עס וועט יא זיין אנגענריים אויף פסח, צי ניט—ריין
מאכען דארף מען".—א סצענע אויף אן ארימען אידישען הויף, אין ווארשא, ערב־
פסח־צייט: מען לופטערט די וואשגעגען דאם בעמגעוואנט א. א. וו.

Airing the bedding and cleaning house for Passover. In preparation for this holiday, Jews remove all traces of leaven and during the holiday period eat unleavened bread like that prepared on the flight from Egypt. Photographer: Alter Kacyzne/*Forward* Art Section, March 21, 1926

Rabbi Binyomin Graubart, with teachers and students of the Mizrachi Talmud Torah on Lag ba'Omer, Staszów, 1930s. Lag ba'Omer is a spring festival commemorating the revolt led by Bar Kokhba against the Romans. Children traditionally carry bows and arrows or toy guns on this holiday.

...AND WORK

From the thirteenth century to the eve of World War II, Jewish merchants and artisans played a special role in the economic life of Poland, which was primarily an agricultural country. Jews were represented in almost every craft, from tailoring and shoemaking to metalworking and smithing. In some occupations—hatmaking, manufacturing of sewing notions and trimmings, brassworking, gold- and tin-smithing, glazing, and the manufacture of fur and other garments—even after World War I, they constituted from seventy-five to one hundred percent of those employed. In these trades, as in baking and butchering, they served both Christian and Jewish populations. Within the Jewish community they were the sole suppliers of baked goods, meat, and garments, inasmuch as these products had to be prepared in accordance with religious law.

Members of the butchers' guild. Tarnów, 1904.

Naftole Grinband, a clockmaker. Góra Kalwaria (Yiddish: *Ger*), 1928. Photographer: Alter Kacyzne/ Raphael Abramovitch Collection

Khone Szlajfer, 85-year-old grinder, umbrella maker, and folk doctor. Łomża, 1927. Photographer: Alter Kacyzne/Raphael Abramovitch Collection

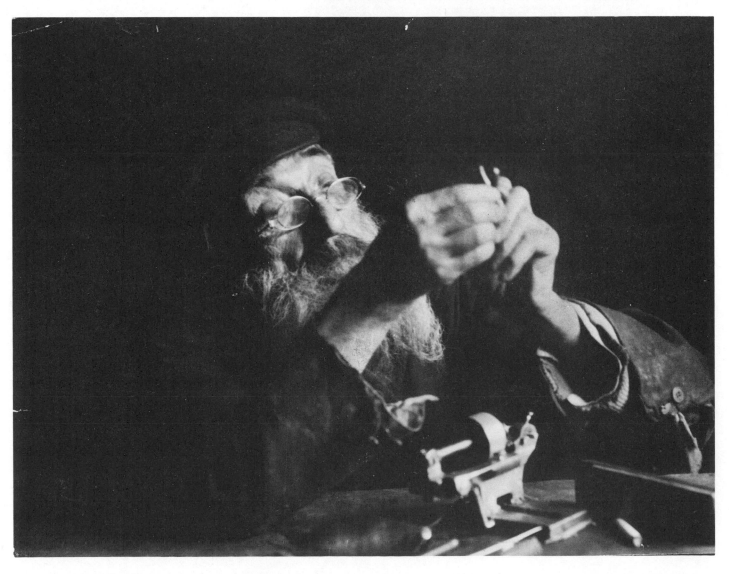

Yisroel Lustman, weaver of peasant linen in Wąwolnica. Photographer: Alter Kacyzne

Zelig, the tailor in Wołomin. Photographer: Alter Kaczyne/Raphael Abramovitch Collection

Shoemaker. Warsaw, 1927. Photographer: Alter Kacyzne/Raphael Abramovitch Collection

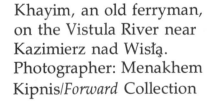

Chairmender in Vilna. Postcard

Watercarrier in Staszów, ca. 1935. His father and grandfather were also watercarriers. Photographer: Avrom Yosl Rotenberg family/Simkhe Rotenberg Collection

Khayim, an old ferryman, on the Vistula River near Kazimierz nad Wisłą. Photographer: Menakhem Kipnis/*Forward* Collection

Sime Świeca, a feather plucker, in Kosów. Feathers, especially goose down, were highly valued, and bedding made from them usually formed part of the dowry. Photographer: Alter Kacyzne/*Forward* Art Section, June 5, 1927

Woman spinning cord, 1938. She is making cord for *tsitses*, the knotted tassels attached to the four corners of the *arbekanfes* (undergarment worn by Orthodox males) and to the *tales* (prayer shawl). Photographer: Roman Vishniac

C. Nachumowski, the Jewish proprietress of an inn. Lubcza, 1930s. Shown with her family and a guest, Dr. Jacob Wygodski, a Zionist leader and member of the Polish Parliament.

Jews and peasant on market day in Otwock, 1937.

Zisl, the street musician. Staszów, 1930s. Photographer: Avrom Yosl Rotenberg family/Simkhe Rotenberg Collection

Klezmorim—traditional musicians, most of them members of the Faust family. Rohatyn, 1912. *Klezmorim* frequently appeared with a *badkhn* (traditional wedding jester), who improvised humorous and sentimental rhymes.

Jewish musicians at a Polish wedding in Łachwa. *Forward* Art Section, January 9, 1927

Berl Cyn, age 87, the oldest blacksmith in the town. Nowe Miasto (Yiddish: *Nayshtot*), 1925. Photographer: L. Przedecki/Raphael Abramovitch Collection

Polish chimney sweep—a well-known character in the Jewish quarter in Pacanów, 1934. Photographer: A. Herszkowicz

In old Poland, legal restrictions almost entirely denied Jews the right to own land and to hold even minor positions in the Polish government bureaucracy. The majority of Jews were employed in urban crafts and commerce. Banned from the Christian guilds, Jewish craftsmen organized their own guilds, which were under the jurisdiction of the local kehillahs.

Later, it was hard for Jewish workers to find employment in big factories. They were entirely banned from certain industries, for example, railroads and mining. Besides, they themselves were reluctant to enter the large-industry factory system; among other reasons, the requirements of the Jewish Sabbath made it impossible for them to comply with the six-day work week. Most Jews continued to work in small workshops, owned and operated by themselves or other Jews, or in a system of cottage industry, much as they had done for centuries.

Part Three
The Camera as Chronicler

CZARIST RUSSIA–
"THE PRISON HOUSE
OF NATIONS"

After Poland was partitioned at the end of the eighteenth century, its eastern territories were incorporated into the Russian empire. For the Jewish population, these areas, known as the Pale of Settlement, were the only part of Russia in which they were permitted to live. Following the Napoleonic wars, central Poland, including the major cities of Warsaw, Łódź, and Lublin with their large Jewish populations, also fell under Russian rule. But central Poland was allowed to maintain a quasi-autonomous status. This area became known as Congress Poland.

All ethnic groups that lived within Russian-dominated territories were deprived of self-determination and of civil and political rights. The Czars' policies toward the Jews, however, were especially severe, contradictory, and changeable. The consistent goal of their policy was to undermine Jewish communal institutions and destroy Jewish national identity. Thus the Czars stripped the kehillah of much of its power and restricted its official role to gathering taxes and supplying Jewish conscripts; they encouraged assimilation through such means as compulsory military service, government-controlled schooling, and bans on traditional dress. At the same time, they encouraged Jews to enter the "more useful" agricultural pursuits and limited opportunities for higher education and for entry into the professions. On occasion, the regime accused Jews of revolutionary or otherwise treasonable acts and encouraged religious fanaticism among the gentile population in order to divert attention from its own misgovernment.

In spite of these repressive acts, Jews managed not only to preserve their traditional institutions but to create a modern

1

2

national literature, press, and theater. They founded social and political movements. They also contributed to the political and intellectual life of Polish and Russian society.

1 Moyshe Tolpin, teacher in a government school, with his family. Ostróg, 1906. Government schools for Jews were established by Czarist edict in 1844 to combat the influence of the *kheyder* and yeshivah and to promote assimilation. While non-Jews supervised the curriculum and taught most general subjects, Jews were sometimes allowed to teach secular subjects. The religious curriculum was taught by Jewish instructors. Although only a small number of Jewish children actually attended them, the new schools opened the way to a broadened and secularized concept of Jewish education and attracted teachers such as the Jewish intellectuals and writers Chaim Zelig Słonimski and Abraham Ber Gotlober. Studio: Rekord

2 A Czarist regiment in Brańsk, 1910. An X indicates Zagelbojm, a Jew in the Czarist army. Until 1827, Jews were not allowed to serve in the Russian army. After this date, Jewish men and boys were inducted into military units—the boys to serve for twenty-five years in the Cantonist Regiments, far from their families and communities. The kehillahs, responsible for supplying conscripts for these regiments, recruited mainly poor boys and those without official residence papers. Occasionally Jewish *khapers* ("snatchers") were employed to kidnap children to fill the quotas. The leadership of the kehillahs was compromised by these practices. Even after 1857, when the Cantonist Regiments were abolished, Jewish soldiers were compelled to serve in the army for exceptionally long periods.

THE REVOLUTION OF 1905

The Revolution of 1905 began in St. Petersburg on January 9, during a peaceful demonstration led by Hapon, a Greek Orthodox priest. The crowd, carrying banners and icons and singing religious songs, was fired on by squads of police and soldiers. After this day, which came to be known as Bloody Sunday, peaceful demonstrations were abandoned.

Casualties of the Bloody Sabbath pogrom in Białystok, 1905.

The anti-Czarists were demanding democratic elections, recognition of workers' rights, cultural autonomy for national minorities, and other political and civil rights. These broad aims were consistent with the goals of the Jewish national and labor movements. Radical Jews in Russia, Congress Poland, and Galicia joined arms with other anti-Czarists and socialists.

When Czar Nicholas II saw that the workers were prepared to wrest their rights by force, he issued a manifesto on October 17 in which he promised to create a constitutional monarchy. At the same time, Czarist authorities instigated pogroms in various parts of the empire in order to divert the masses and to divide the anti-Czarist forces.

By the end of 1906, the revolution had subsided. In 1907, a wave of repression and a determined program of Russification followed the appointment of Stolypin as Minister of the Interior. Hundreds of revolutionaries were executed, thousands were exiled to Siberia, and many fled the country. To this day, Jews who left Russia and Poland for Palestine between 1907 and 1911 refer to their emigration as the Stolypin Aliyah.

Striking weavers in front of the Wiślicki factory. Łódź, 1902.

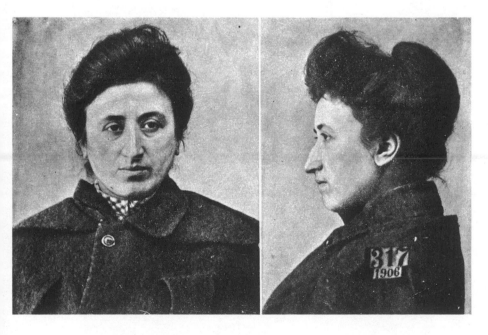

Rosa Luxemburg, theoretician and leader of the Polish and German revolutionary movements, in the Warsaw jail in 1906. An organizer of the Revolution of 1905, Rosa Luxemburg was arrested by the Czarist police. After she escaped from jail in 1906, she went to Germany and became the founder of the Spartakus party, the leftist organization that was the predecessor of the German Communist Party. She and Karl Liebknecht were murdered while being transferred to the Moabit jail in Berlin.

1

2

1 Polish and Russian Social Democrats and members of the Bund *(Algemeyner yidisher arbeter bund in lite, poyln, un rusland),* honoring the victims of the October 1905 pogrom in Vilna.

2 Mass demonstration for universal suffrage, Tarnów 1905, organized by Polish and Jewish socialist parties. The signs declare "We Demand a General Election."

Political prisoners, 1907. Studio: L. M. Gelgor, Grodno

THE GREAT WAR, 1914–1918

Long before the first shot had been fired, the powers of Europe had aligned themselves on opposing sides; the Central Powers (Germany and Austria-Hungary) were in conflict with the Allies (France, Russia, and Great Britain) over spheres of influence and territory in Europe, Africa, and Asia. The assassination of Grand Duke Franz Ferdinand on June 28, 1914, in Sarajevo, sparked the outbreak of World War I. From the outset, Germany was forced to fight at the same time against France on the west and Russia on the east. The three major areas of Jewish settlement—Congress Poland, Galicia, and the Pale of Jewish Settlement—were the scene of battle on the eastern front.

The destruction of Mińsk Street, Smorgonie. Almost the entire town was demolished in World War I.

Living conditions in Poland during World War I. Gustav Eisner Collection

Soup kitchen for Jewish children in Warsaw, established with the financial assistance of the Great Britain–Poland Association.

Khayim Ślafak of Świsłocz, known as Khayim the baker—one of 400,000 Jewish soldiers in the Russian army during World War I. Ironically, while some Jews were suspected of treachery by the Russians and were deported or killed, other Jews served in the Russian army and found themselves fighting Jews enlisted in opposing armies. Avrom Ain Collection

Anna Sedlis, a Jewish nurse, who served in the Russian army during the war with her husband, Elias, a medical doctor.

After indecisive initial encounters, the Germans forced the Russians to retreat along the northern and central fronts. However, the Russian army managed to advance against the Austro-Hungarians and penetrated deep into Galicia. About 400,000 Jews fled to the western part of Galicia and to Austria proper; most of them escaped before the army approached. A wave of pogroms began, as Lwów, Złoczów, Gródek Jagielloński, and other towns and cities fell into Russian hands. During their short stay in eastern Galicia, the Russians deprived Jews of civil rights granted under Franz Josef, the Austrian emperor, removed them from elected positions in municipal councils and courts, and dissolved their institutions of self-government.

Similarly, on the northern front, the Russians deported deep into Russia tens of thousands of Jews from the provinces of Grodno, Kovno, Vilna, Suwałki, and Białystok who were suspected of being enemy sympathizers and spies—some were accused of communicating with the Germans by means of hidden telephones and of concealing entire regiments of German cavalry. The Jews were blamed for the disgraceful defeats suffered at the hands of the Germans.

In 1915 the Germans broke the Russian defense on the central and northern fronts, forcing the Russians to abandon Vilna, and helped the Austro-Hungarian army push the Russians out of Galicia. From this time, and until the end of the war, the Central Powers controlled Congress Poland, Galicia, and much of the Pale of Jewish Settlement.

THE GERMAN OCCUPATION, 1915-1918

From the day the Germans set foot in Poland, they sought to enlist the support of the population in the war against Russia. Germany, like Austria-Hungary, allowed Józef Piłsudski, leader of the Polish liberation movement, to mobilize the Polish Legions to help fight the Russians. German army posters proclaimed: "Join our forces! In common struggle we will chase the Asian hordes from Poland's borders."* In addition there were special appeals directed to the Jews alone, warning them in Yiddish:

> *Do not let yourselves be misled by false promises! Did not the Czar in 1905 promise equal rights for Jews? How did he fulfill his promise? Remember the expulsions of Jewish masses from their long-established settlements! Remember Kishinev, Homel, Białystok, Siedlce, and hundreds of other bloody pogroms!* †

---

*Jerzy Holzer and Jan Molenda, *Polska w pierwszej wojnie światowej* (Warsaw: Wiedza Powszechna, 1967), p. 50.

†*Tsu di yidn in poyln* (handbill), Vilna Collection, YIVO Institute for Jewish Research Archives.

German officers ride into the Jewish
quarter of Mława, 129 kilometers
northwest of Warsaw, 1914. Studio:
Hofphotograph Kühlewindt, Königs-
berg, Prussia/ Postcard: Kunstanstalt
J. Themal, Posen

Jewish merchants pose with
Austro-Hungarian officers in
a photographer's studio.
Dęblin, 1916.

Flanked by two German soldiers, boys sell the *Wilnaer Zeitung*. The newspaper was issued by the Germans, who occupied Vilna on September 18, 1915. Ephim H. Jeshurin Collection

Children holding sheet music while a German military brass band plays victory marches. Unidentified newspaper clipping/Gustav Eisner Collection

German soldiers seek lodging in a Jewish house.

"Wenn die Soldaten durch die Stadt marschieren,
Offnen die Mädchen die Fenster und Türen.
Warum? Ach, darum . . ."

(When the soldiers march through the city,
The girls open the windows and doors.
Why? Ah, because . . .)

German soldier's song
World War I

Unidentified newspaper clipping/Gustav Eisner
Collection

Germans search for smuggled food at a
checkpoint in Częstochowa, 1914. Gustav Eisner Collection/From *Das Generalgouvernement Warschau* (Oldenburg:
Verlag des deutschen Offizierblattes,
1918), p. 158

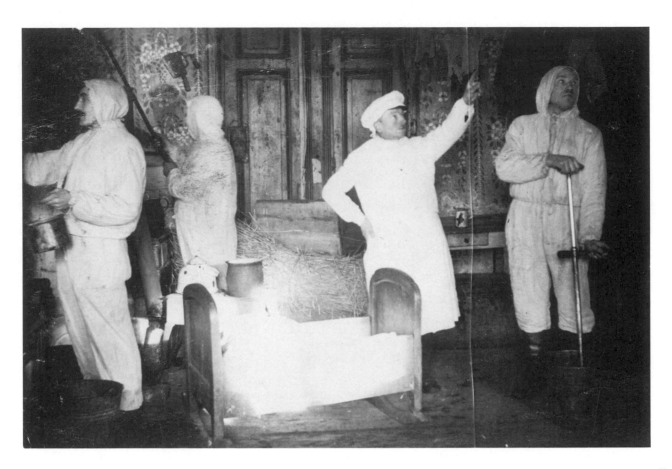

Germans disinfecting living quarters in an effort to control infectious diseases, especially typhus.

"Aufstehen, Frühstück machen, und zum Bad gehen"

(Arise, make breakfast, and bathe)

German army saying
World War I

Gustav Eisner Collection

The Germans saw the Jews as natural allies in the war and in the postwar order they hoped to establish in Poland. German Jews, who felt compassion for the plight of the East European Jews, encouraged the German government to liberate them from the Russian yoke. As a result of German policy in the occupied territories, Polish Jews enjoyed more liberty than they had ever experienced under the Czar. With the moral and financial support of German Jewry and of Jewish communities throughout the world, they began to rebuild their communal institutions and to restore their economic and cultural life, in spite of wartime conditions and the restrictions imposed on them by a foreign military government.

Feldrabbiner Dr. Sali Lewi of Breslau. Lewi was one of many Jewish chaplains in the German army during World War I. With permission from the German government and funds from the Breslau Jewish community, he helped Jews in the Vilna area to recover from the effects of the war and to revive their communal life. Through his efforts, a school of agriculture and animal husbandry was established.

Dr. Lewi prepared a report for the Breslau *Verein für jüdische Geschichte und Literatur*, describing his activities among the Jews in the Vilna area during the war and illustrated with photographs.

On a municipal election day in the Jewish quarter in Częstochowa during World War I. Campaigners went from courtyard to courtyard carrying placards. One placard read:

"Voters! Hurry to City Hall to vote. Remember that S. S. [Polish abbreviation for Socialist-Zionist] is Number One [on the ballot]."

Studio: Apollo/Gustav Eisner Collection

THE REBIRTH OF THE POLISH REPUBLIC, 1918

Poland regained her independence in 1918. The three monarchies that ruled her for almost one hundred and fifty years were overthrown: Czarist Russia in the Revolution of 1917 and Germany and Austria-Hungary as a result of their defeat by the Allies, who were joined by the United States in 1917. In his Fourteen Points, President Wilson said: "An independent Polish state should be erected . . . whose territorial integrity [is] guaranteed by international covenant."

On November 11, 1918, the very day that Germany accepted the terms of the armistice, the Polish Legions under

Józef Piłsudski disarmed the German troops and proclaimed the independence of Poland. Jews had fought in Piłsudski's Polish Legions from their inception, served as high-ranking officers, and held important posts in their civil branches. Just as they had participated in previous Polish national liberation movements—from the Kościuszko revolt of 1794 to the uprising of January 1863—Jews fought for Polish liberation in 1918.

At the Peace Conference in Versailles in 1919, the Allies officially recognized Polish sovereignty on condition that Poland abide by the minority-protection clauses appended to the Treaty of Versailles. Representatives of European and American Jewish organizations, including the lawyer and communal leader Louis Marshall, had fought for the national-minority clauses, which granted full political and civil rights, religious freedom, and cultural autonomy to Poland's national minorities. These provisions were guaranteed by the League of Nations and were incorporated into the Polish Constitution of 1921.

1 Two fighters for Polish independence. Warsaw, 1916. Henryk Barwiński, actor and director, in the uniform of the Polish Legions, with his uncle Leon Hertz, who fought in the Polish national uprising against Russia in 1863.

2 Henry Morgenthau, flanked by American officers. Poland, 1919. Morgenthau headed a commission sent by President Wilson to investigate anti-Semitic pogroms and the conditions of the Jews in the newly formed Republic. Studio: Broudner, Vilna/Gustav Eisner Collection

1

2

A colony of houses, schools, and workshops (exterior and interior views) built by the American Joint Distribution Committee in Brześć nad Bugiem (Yiddish: *Brisk*). It was named The Felix Warburg Colony in honor of the distinguished president of the Committee.

THE POLISH-RUSSIAN WAR, 1920

The last day of war is rarely the first day of peace. In the spring of 1920, friction between Soviet Russia and Poland erupted in a full-scale war. In May, after a brief campaign, the Poles advanced as far as Kiev, where the Red Army repulsed them. After launching a counterattack, the Red Army reached the banks of the Vistula on August 14. On the following day, Józef Piłsudski led the Polish army in a massive offensive, later called the "Miracle on the Vistula," in which they broke the Russian advance. The Polish army then drove the Russians out of Poland.

A family of war refugees finds shelter in the women's section of a synagogue in Brześć nad Bugiem.

Jews in the Fourth Regiment of the Polish army near Vilna celebrate Rosh Hashanah, 1920. This food kitchen was maintained by the kehillah of Nowa Wilejka.

The majority of the Jewish population supported the Polish effort and tens of thousands of Jewish men and women served in regular military units on the front lines. However, some political parties, the Bund among them, called the war an imperialistic war. They opposed it in principle. Some groups—Communists and other extreme leftists—were sympathetic to the Bolsheviks.

The Polish rightists used any indication of Jewish support for the Bolsheviks as a pretext for a campaign against Jewish soldiers and in order to incite riots against the civilian Jewish population. Ironically, even some Jews who had been ardent supporters of Piłsudski and had fought for Polish independence were among those affected by this wave of anti-Semitism.

Marshal Józef Piłsudski is offered bread and salt by the Jewish community in Dęblin after he captured the town from the Bolsheviks in August, 1920. His signature appears on the photograph. Photographer: M. Fuks/I. Perle Collection

Members of a women's regiment in the Polish army celebrate the first anniversary of the capture of the city of Lwów from the Ukrainians, a battle in which they took part. *Forward* Collection

A Russian soldier talks to a Jewish member of the local revolutionary government established by the Red Army and Polish Communist Party. Grajewo, 1920. *Forward* Collection

Jewish soldiers and officers in the Polish army who had fought for Polish independence and who were later interned because it was feared that they might support the enemy. This incident raised heated protest in the Polish Parliament and the men were later released and exonerated. Jabłonna, 1920.

JEWS
AS POLISH
CITIZENS

The Jews were perhaps the only Polish minority whose interests did not conflict with Polish sovereignty or the integrity of her borders. In an address delivered in the Polish Parliament on February 24, 1919, in response to anti-Semitic speeches from rightist members, Izaak Grünbaum, leader of the Zionist party, said:

> We greet the rebirth of the united and independent Polish Republic with the greatest joy. . . . As citizens of the Polish state, equal in rights and obligations, we wish to work most zealously in the reconstruction of a free, powerful, and happy Poland, which will base its existence and growth on justice, democracy, and equality for all its citizens. . . . Do not rebuff the efforts of three million citizens to cooperate in the reconstruction of the Polish state. Give us such conditions that a Polish Jew anywhere in the world may proudly proclaim Civis Polonus sum et nihil civitatis Poloniae a me alienum puto [I am a Polish citizen and nothing pertaining to the Polish state is foreign to me].*

By virtue of the minority-protection clauses of the Treaty of Versailles and the Polish Constitution of 1921, Jews were granted equal rights and cultural autonomy. The representative political system of Poland did allow for the election of many Jews to both houses of Parliament and to municipal councils, although their access to appointed positions in the government was limited. Almost all Jewish political parties and social groups were represented on many levels of elective office.

*I. Schiper, A. Tartakower, and A. Hafftka, eds., Żydzi w Polsce Odrodzonej: Działalność społeczna, gospodarcza, oświatowa i kulturalna, vol. 2 (Warsaw: Żydzi w Polsce Odrodzonej, [1932–1933]), p. 315.

Voters line up at the polls in a Jewish neighborhood in
Warsaw to elect representatives to the Polish Parliament.
Photographer: Alter Kacyzne/*Forward* Collection

Eight of the thirteen Jewish representatives in the first Polish
Parliament in 1919. They included members of the Orthodox,
Populist, and Zionist parties. *Forward* Collection

Róża Pomerantz-Meltzer, Zionist and member of the Polish Parliament. *Forward* Collection

Professor Mojżesz Schorr visiting Brześć nad Bugiem in the 1930s. Schorr, an Assyriologist and historian and rabbi of the Tłomackie Synagogue in Warsaw, was a Zionist and member of the Polish Parliament.

S. Kaufer, mayor of the village Jeziorany Żydowskie (Jewish Jeziorany). His badge and hat bear insignias of his office. *Nasz Przegląd*, November 4, 1928

דער ערשטער יודישער ראטמענער צוזאמענפאר אין פוילען

The first national convention of Jewish municipal representatives in Poland. Dobrzyń nad Wisłą. Izaak Grünbaum is seated in the center of the front row.

"In weight a fly, in strength a lion." Łazar Rundsztein, flyweight boxing champion of Poland, 1937. *Yidishe bilder*, August 1938

Boys' and girls' classrooms in a government school for Jews (*Szabasówka*) in Warsaw. The name *Szabasówka*, derived from the word for "Sabbath," was used because Jews were allowed to close their schools on Saturday.

EMIGRATION

Migration and resettlement within Europe were constant elements in East European life. Migration to the New World began at the time of the American Revolution. It remained limited in scale until well into the nineteenth century, when economic upheavals, wars, revolutions and the reactions that followed them caused waves of immigrants to seek a better life in the land of opportunity—the fabulous "Golden Land."

During the years 1880–1914, more than one and a half million Jews left Congress Poland, the Pale of Settlement, and Galicia. Seventy percent of those who emigrated went to the United States. In Galicia, where industry was almost nonexistent, extreme poverty persuaded them to leave. In the Pale of Settlement and Congress Poland, which were under Russian control, severe economic hardship was attended by periods of repressive legislation, anti-Jewish boycotts, and pogroms.

The greatest wave of emigration from independent Poland occurred in the aftermath of World War I and the Polish-Russian War of 1920. In 1921, the last year of open immigration to the United States, almost 75,000 Jews left Poland. As a result of legislation introduced in that year, large-scale immigration to the United States was virtually ended by 1924. Other countries adopted the same closed-door policy, especially after the onset of the Depression in 1929. Although immigration to Palestine also was restricted by the British White Papers, it was not entirely suspended; roughly half the Jews who left Poland between 1921 and 1939 settled in Palestine.

From the first days of Poland's independence, in 1918, Jewish political parties fought for the *right* to emigrate (the Zionists made it one of their chief demands), but they fought against having this right converted into an obligation. Polish rightist and extremist factions, however, strenuously advocated a policy of forced Jewish emigration. In the Parliament and press and on the streets, the cry was raised: "Jews to Palestine! Jews to Madagascar!" In the late thirties, the Polish government itself advocated Jewish mass emigration.

HIAS

HIAS (Hebrew Immigrant Aid Society) maintained a branch office in Warsaw. In cooperation with the American Joint Distribution Committee and other organizations, HIAS assisted Jews from all parts of Poland to travel to Warsaw and provided them with room and board during the weeks it took to clear their papers through the embassies, undergo medical examinations, and book their passage.

These photographs, selected from the more than one hundred taken by Alter Kacyzne in 1921, show aspects of the emigration process as it was facilitated by HIAS.

HIAS office messenger.

At the
information
desk.

In the front
courtyard of
the HIAS
building—
after receiving
their emigra-
tion papers.

Receiving a loan. The large sums in the list of debts posted on the wall reflect the depreciation of Polish currency at the time—in June 1921 one dollar bought 2,923 Polish marks.

The HIAS dining room.

The Red Star-American Line shipping office in Warsaw.

In Warsaw, waiting to leave for the port in the Free City of Gdańsk (Danzig).

Freight train carrying emigrants to Gdańsk. A stove is visible through the open door.

Passenger train
to Gdańsk.

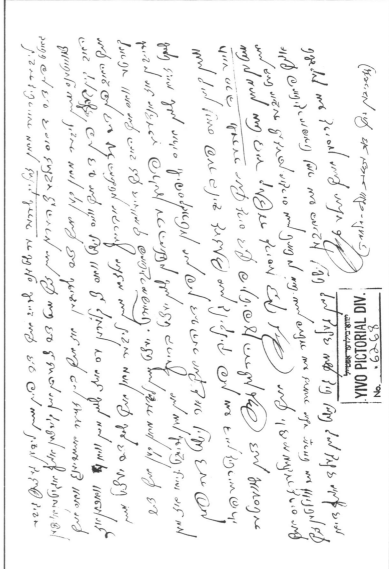

Khaye Sore Szerer. After World War I, Khaye Sore Szerer sent a photograph to her husband, Zelig, who had emigrated to America. On the back she wrote in Yiddish:

To my dear, devoted husband Zelig Szerer. First, I write to you of my good health and hope to God that I may hear the same from you and see you soon in good shape. Second, my dear husband, I can write you that I am very worried that I have no letter from you. I don't know what to think. It is already more than four weeks since I received a letter from you. And so, my dear husband, I am sending you my photograph, which I had taken this week. Now, my dear husband, I can write you that other women are already receiving letters, and they are told that they are being sent steamship tickets, and from you I hear nothing about it. No more news. Stay healthy and happy. From me, your devoted wife, Khaye Sore Szerer. I send you regards from the bottom of my heart. Regards to your sister and her husband. And the children send regards. We are all alright. We would have had all of us photographed, but we have no money. We don't get any money for the checks. We all send you our love.

Studio: "Rembrandt," Zamość

THE CRITICAL DECADES

The first parliamentary governments in the Second Polish Republic were composed of right-wing and centrist elements. They faced a country in ruins after six years of war. Obstructed by a strong and factious Parliament, they sought unsuccessfully to establish a stable currency, create jobs for millions of unemployed workers and landless peasants, and find a *modus vivendi* with Poland's national minorities and with neighboring states. Popular discontent grew and was expressed in a series of strikes, mass demonstrations, and riots.

Gabriel Narutowicz, first President of the Polish Republic, was the target of a campaign waged by rightists and nationalists. He was called the "Jewish President" because the

President Narutowicz on his way to the Parliament to take the oath of office on December 11, 1922—five days later he was assassinated. From *Gabrjel Narutowicz, pierwszy prezydent Rzeczypospolitej: Księga pamiątkowa* (Warsaw: Komitet Uczczenia Pierwszego Prezydenta RP, 1925), p. 231

Soldiers suppress a workers' attempt to overthrow the Wincenty Witos government. Cracow, November 6, 1923. *Forward* Collection

deciding votes in his election in the Parliament were cast by representatives of the national minorities, who included Jews. He was assassinated on December 16, 1922, by Eligiusz Niewiadomski, an extreme rightist.

Piłsudski withdrew from political life in 1922 in protest against the absence of effective leadership in the government of Poland. In 1926, supported by a majority of the armed forces, the populace, and the opposition political parties, he effected a dramatic *coup d'état.* The Jews and other national minorities strongly backed Piłsudski not only because he sought to remedy the ills of the previous regime but because of his federalist stand, which promised solutions to the problems

Piłsudski's troops on guard in front of the railroad station in Warsaw during the *coup d'état* in May 1926. *Forward* Collection

In the Jewish cemetery in Warsaw, a military company honors Jewish soldiers who died fighting on Piłsudski's side in 1926. Photographer: Menakhem Kipnis/Raphael Abramovitch Collection

Cwi Tenenbaum, a Jewish soldier in the Polish army stationed in Bydgoszcz, 1928. A rabbinical student, he was given special permission to wear a beard. *Nasz Przegląd*, September 30, 1928

Jew whose beard was cut off by Polish soldiers. Łódź, 1923. Gustav Eisner Collection

Demonstration of 50,000 Warsaw Jews protesting British restrictions on Jewish immigration to Palestine. Photographer: H. Bojm/*Nasz Przegląd*, June 15, 1930

of the minorities. Piłsudski's government succeeded in many ways but failed to resolve the basic issues. Disillusioned by his attempts to undermine the parliamentary system, some of his strongest supporters, including the Polish Socialist party, joined the opposition.

After Piłsudski died in 1935, his successors acknowledged equal rights for Jews in theory but gradually undermined those rights in practice. Outside the government, extremists incited pogroms and harassment of Jews. Quotas *(numerus clausus)* and "ghetto benches," which segregated Jews in classrooms, were introduced in many universities. Such events produced feelings of disquiet and concern among Polish liberals, many of whom provided moral and political support to the Jews in this difficult time.

Shop of Jankielewicz the watchmaker, in the Jewish quarter of Grodno. The shop was looted in the pogrom of June, 1935. *Forward* Collection

Family injured during the pogrom in Mińsk Mazowiecki in June, 1936.
Photographer: Żychliński/*Forward* Collection

Wacław Szumański, a Polish
lawyer who defended Jews at
the trial following the Przytyk
pogrom.

Policeman arrests Leyzer Feldberg,
a 70-year-old Jew who fought with
the rioters during the infamous
pogrom in Przytyk in March, 1936.
Forward Collection

Members of the Jewish self-defense group in Przytyk stand by while bread is distributed.

THE ZBĄSZYN AFFAIR AND "KRISTALLNACHT"

Nazi Germany issued one hundred and twenty-three anti-Jewish decrees and regulations during the three years between September 1935, when the Nuremberg Laws were passed, and October 1938, when the first mass deportation of Jews occurred. In October 1938, the Germans expelled about fifteen thousand Jews who were Polish citizens residing in Germany. At first, Poland did not allow them to reenter the country, and they remained trapped in no-man's-land or held in the border town of Zbąszyn. The deportees were allowed entry only after

Jewish refugees from Germany gather in Zbąszyn, on the German-Polish border. *Forward* Collection

international public opinion was aroused and protests were voiced in Poland by Jews and by Polish liberal circles.

Hershl Grynszpan, a student in Paris whose parents were among those expelled, sought revenge on the Germans by shooting Ernst vom Rath, a Nazi official in the German Embassy. The Nazis used this incident as a pretext for ordering anti-Jewish riots all over Germany, beginning in Berlin on November 8/9, 1938, later known as *Kristallnacht* (Night of Broken Glass). Thirty-six Jews were murdered, hundreds injured, and thousands arrested. Jewish stores and houses were looted and destroyed and synagogues were set on fire. All through the night the Nazis publicly stoked bonfires with piles of books, most of them by Jewish authors. They included the works of Heinrich Heine, who once said, "When books are burned, it is a sign that people will be burned too."

THE EVE OF WORLD WAR II

On January 22, 1933, the day they seized control of Germany, the Nazis embarked on their campaign against the Jews and began preparations for the conquest of Europe. In 1938, the German army moved with a centrifugal force that eventually extended east, west, north, and south. Its first victims were Austria and the Sudetenland of Czechoslovakia. In the spring of 1939, the Germans took the remainder of Bohemia-Moravia and the province of Memel, a territory in Lithuania, without firing a shot. This was the time of the Munich policy of appeasement.

On September 1, 1939, nine days after Molotov and Ribbentrop signed the Nazi-Soviet nonaggression pact in Moscow, Germany invaded Poland and defeated her in a short but fierce struggle. The invasion of Poland marked the beginning of World War II, which was to last a total of 2,076 days. During that time, most of the East European Jewish community was destroyed. In Poland alone, three million Jews were annihilated.

Arms outstretched in the Nazi salute, Colonial Germans *(Volksdeutschen)* parade in Warsaw in 1938. Photographer: Roman Vishniac

1

1 Swastikas and German eagles decorate the main street of the Free City of Gdańsk (Danzig). Most of the residents were Germans. After 1933, the local Nazis controlled the city. *Forward* Collection

2 The Przeworski family and Polish officers on the Warsaw airfield in 1938, in front of one of the planes which the family, who were owners of several sugar refineries, gave to the Polish army.

3 A demonstration of Poland's readiness and determination to fight the Germans. Warsaw, March 20, 1939. *Forward* Collection

2

3

Wehrmacht unit crosses the Polish border on September 1, 1939—the beginning of World War II. From Tadeusz Kułakowski, *Gdyby Hitler zwyciężył*. . . . (Warsaw: Książka i Wiedza, 1960)

German soldiers en route to Poland in September 1939. The slogan emblazoned on the train reads:

"Wir fahren nach Polen um Juden zu versohlen"
(We're going to Poland to beat up the Jews)

Part Four
Creating a Modern Existence

THE CITY

With the migration of Jews to larger towns and metropolitan centers, old social ties and the cohesiveness of traditional communities were weakened. These factors intensified conflicts between generations that had been created by the challenge to traditional values posed by the Haskalah (Jewish Enlightenment) and its westernizing and secularizing influence.

The transformation of Jewish life in the middle of the nineteenth century was also a response to the gradual removal of legal restrictions in various parts of partitioned Poland and to radical changes in the economic structure. Thus, with the liberation of the serfs, millions of landless peasants flooded the labor market. Many of them moved to towns and cities, where they created a new class of urban factory workers that competed with Jewish craftsmen but that also provided labor for a small but influential Jewish and non-Jewish upper middle class of factory owners and industrialists. Although legally free to live where they wished, to engage in most occupations, and to enter universities, Jews faced increasing economic hardship and also moved to towns and cities. By 1931, about 750,000 Jews, a full twenty-five percent of Poland's Jewish population, lived in the country's five largest cities—Warsaw, Łódź, Vilna, Cracow, and Lwów. Indeed, the Jewish community in Warsaw became the largest in Europe.

Although Jews living in cities and towns still encountered obstacles to their social and economic mobility, they were able to create an active Jewish cultural life. Each town had its literary circles, drama groups, local library, sports clubs, educational facilities, and political and social organizations. The concern for modernizing Jewish education and making it a means of realizing specific social and political ideals led to the development of many educational alternatives. Indeed, the

Business courtyard on Nalewki Street in the Jewish quarter of Warsaw, 1938. In shops on upper floors and on the street level, living and business quarters were often combined in one space. Photographer: Roman Vishniac

Świętokrzyska Street in Warsaw, where the shops of Jewish dealers in rare books were located.

Policeman in
Warsaw giving
a ticket to a
cyclist. Raphael
Abramovitch
Collection

Courtyard scene in
an apartment house
in Warsaw, 1938.
Photographer: Roman
Vishniac/Raphael
Abramovitch
Collection

At the corner of Ujazdowskie Avenue and Matejki Street in Warsaw, late 1930s. Raphael Abramovitch Collection

Jewish proletariat in large measure constituted an intelligentsia of workers. It provided an enormous readership for a growing popular Yiddish literature and press—before World War II about three thousand Jewish newspapers and magazines were published in Poland—a mass audience for an active Yiddish theater, and the constituency for an increasing number of political and social movements.

Only the largest cities, however, supported the full range of cultural and political institutions and activities—sustained, for example, fifteen Yiddish theater companies in one season (as was the case in Vilna in 1935), served as the home of the most distinguished literary circles, such as that of Peretz in Warsaw, and as the center for Jewish political and social organizations. In large cities, Jews attended Jewish institutes for higher learning and Polish universities, joined Polish cultural and intellectual circles, and were exposed to cosmopolitan lifestyles and values that influenced Jewish life throughout Poland.

WORKERS, SHOPKEEPERS, INDUSTRIALISTS

Industrial development in Eastern Europe proceeded at a relatively slow and uneven pace without seriously changing the basically agricultural character of the region. The more rapid industrialization of Congress Poland and the Polish provinces of the Pale was stimulated by the availability of raw materials and a market for manufactured goods in the vast and largely undeveloped Russian empire. It was thus possible, for example, for Łódź, as a result of its burgeoning textile industry, to

Factory roofs in the great manufacturing and textile city of Łódź, called the "Polish Manchester." Józef Piłsudski Institute Collection

Brandsteter's clothing factory. Tarnów, 1910.

grow in two generations from a village to the second largest city in Congress Poland.

While expanding the economic opportunities of Jewish workers and small entrepreneurs, industrialization and the development of a market economy also eliminated some traditional areas of Jewish economic activity and created an economic crisis in small towns, whose role had been circumscribed by the competitive market system. Jews migrated to urban centers (and to Western Europe and America) in search of employment. There they entered the industrial sector as entrepreneurs, workers, and managers.

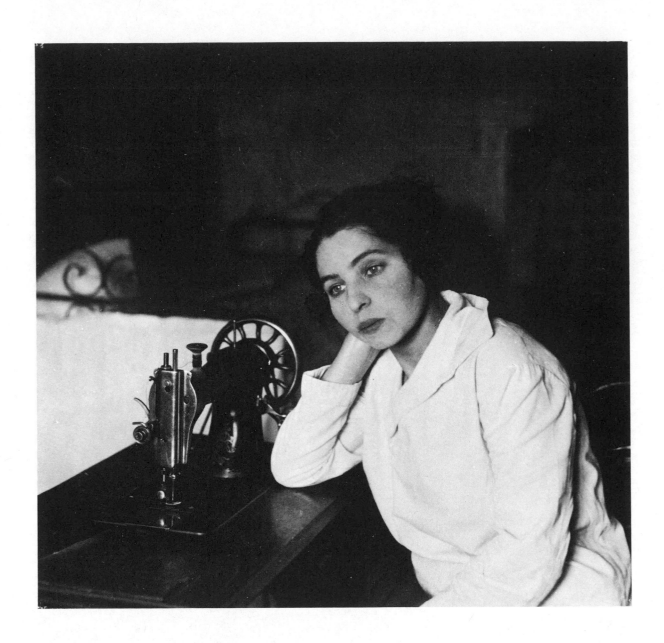

Unemployed seamstress sitting beside her Singer sewing machine. Białystok, 1926. Photographer: Alter Kacyzne/Raphael Abramovitch Collection

Only a very few Jews became large-scale entrepreneurs (although these constituted a substantial percentage of all major industrialists in Poland). A small number came from banking families—the Kronenbergs, Epsteins, and Wawelbergs. Most rose from the lower middle class—Y. K. Poznański, the textile tycoon of Łódź, began as a clerk in a factory; Józef Szereszewski, the greatest tobacco industrialist in Eastern Europe, had started as a shopkeeper. Most Jewish entrepreneurs, however, were involved in small-scale industry; many of them had also begun as merchants and craftsmen, often as part of the cottage industry system which served large-scale industry.

1 Hipolit Wawelberg (1843–1901), industrialist, banker, philanthropist, and patron of arts and letters.

2 Ludwika Wawelberg, wife of Hipolit Wawelberg and daughter of the art collector and historian Matthias Bersohn.

2

Ignacy Mościcki, President of the Polish Republic, visits the Wawelberg summer colony for Polish and Jewish children at Puszcza Kampinoska, 1930. Józef Piłsudski Institute Collection

The stock exchange in Warsaw, in the 1920s. *Forward* Collection

Private fire brigade employed at the tobacco factory of Józef Szereszewski in Grodno.

These successful businessmen in the dress industry in Brzeziny were once poor tailors. Photographer: L. Przedecki/*Forward* Collection

The mansion of Yitskhok K. Poznański, a nineteenth-century textile magnate in Łódź.

Excluded from heavy industry and discouraged from entering large factories, Jewish workers were concentrated in small workshops. In 1921, only fifteen percent of all Jewish workers were engaged in firms employing more than ten workers, whereas fifty percent of Christian workers were in factories engaging more than fifty employees. Jews were engaged primarily in garment manufacture, forestry, food production, and wholesale and retail trade. In the case of the textile, forestry, sugar, and oil industries, they served specialized functions, particularly in management and in the distribution of goods.

In the service area, Jews were prevented from entering the public service sector—central government and municipal services and public transportation. The opening up of the liberal professions and educational opportunities and the expansion of social services within the Jewish community provided Jews, especially those from the middle class, with new avenues for social and economic mobility.

With the formation of independent Poland, Jews found themselves again hampered by discriminatory policies that promoted the interests of the ethnic majority. Government monopolies on the tobacco industry, alcohol distilleries, and match factories were accompanied by the dismissal of most of their Jewish workers. State subsidies to various branches of industry were denied Jews. In the 1930s, mounting anti-Semitism and the general economic crisis in Poland contributed further to the decline of Jewish shopkeepers and the increase in the number of Jewish workers in small factories, where the hours were long, the pay poor, and the layoffs frequent. The number of unemployed increased rapidly. The most formidable weapon employed by the Polish right was the boycott of Jewish goods and shops. Many who did not approve of violence believed the boycotts to be a peaceable solution to the Jewish question and a way to encourage the Jews to emigrate to Palestine, or to Madagascar, or to any place that would receive them.

Delivery wagon on Gęsia Street in the Jewish section of Warsaw, 1938. Signs advertise goods and services available in shops on the street and in the court-yards—homecooked meals, hemstitching and embroidery, and bicycle repairs were among the services offered; goods sold included scissors, razors, umbrellas, furs, underwear, and gramophones. Photographer: Roman Vishniac/Raphael Abramovitch Collection

Moyshe Hochman, deliveryman and bus driver. Nasielsk, 1929. He has replaced his old horse and buggy with an autobus. Photographer: Menakhem Kipnis/*Forward* Art Section, January 27, 1929

Locksmith's workshop in his basement dwelling. Warsaw, 1938. Photographer:
Roman Vishniac

Schoolboy in front of a shop where galoshes and rubber boots are repaired, in Lublin, 1938. Photographer: Roman Vishniac

Glaziers and painters posing before a building. Tarnów, 1908.

THREE MIDDLE-CLASS FAMILIES

The Szabad Family

Three generations of the family of Pesa and Yosef Szabad (seated, center). Vilna, 1897. Pesa Szabad was the daughter of Rabbi Yankev Dovid Pyeshin, head of the Ramailes Yeshivah in Vilna. She kept a shop in Vilna. Her husband, Yosef, was a merchant. Cemach Szabad (standing, back row center), son of Yosef and Pesa, was a prominent physician and a leader of the *Folkist* Party, member of the Polish Parliament, and a founder of the YIVO in Vilna. Photographer: N. Serebrin

The Hirszowicz Family

The Hirszowicz family owned one of the largest printing companies in Poland. Lejba Hirszowicz (1830–1907) was an engraver of silverware for the Russian nobility. His oldest son, Józef, established an engraving and printing plant in Moscow. In 1892 he moved his business to Warsaw, where it prospered. Twenty years later, he built a modern five-story printing plant.

Józef Hirszowicz was active in Jewish communal affairs and was a member of the council of the Tłomackie Synagogue in Warsaw. His children attended private gymnasiums and Polish and foreign universities. They became doctors, lawyers, and engineers, and some of them participated in revolutionary movements in Russia and Poland.

Józef and Dora Hirszowicz, with their eleven children and daughter-in-law. Warsaw, 1904.

Invitation to the wedding.

On the occasion of the wedding of
Miss Marja Joffe
to
Mr. Włodzimierz Hirszowicz
Sunday, November 15, 1903

Wedding menu.

Fish: Rhine Lox in Mayonnaise
with Tartar Sauce
Filet of Beef with Vegetables and Mushroom Sauce
Bouillon with Pastries
Capon, Turkey, Chicken
Squab and Duck
Compote Italienne
Pineapple
Bombe Mexicaine
Dessert
Coffee and Liqueurs

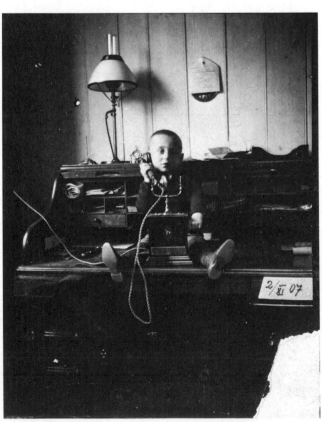

Leon Hirszowicz, son of
Włodzimierz and Marja,
in his grandfather's office.
Warsaw, 1907.

The Rubinlicht Children

Ruta (née Rubinlicht) and Boas Karlíński, with Ruta's sister Bella, brother Henryk, and Der Tunkeler (J. Tunkel). Bella attended the School of Drama in Warsaw. Later she joined the Vilna Troupe and, after 1924, became a star of the American Yiddish theater. Her stage name was Bella Bellarina. Bella and Ruta, who was dentist, were two of twelve gifted children. Their brother Feliks, a sculptor, graduated from the Art Academy in Warsaw. Their sister Halina studied bacteriology and Natalia, the youngest, was a theater designer.

COMMUNAL INSTITUTIONS

Jews had brought to Poland a form of self-government whose basic character had been shaped by Talmudic tradition and whose legal status was dependent on privileges granted them by Polish princes and kings. Jewish communities, like other groups in feudal Poland, were juridical units with legal corporate rights that ensured them a large measure of autonomy in governing themselves according to their own traditions. Each Jewish community, or kehillah, had an executive board composed of officers elected from and by a wealthy and learned elite. The tasks of overall administration and law enforcement fell to the governing board, while judiciary functions were handled in the main by Jewish courts, which administered civil, family, and public law. A rabbi was the appointed spiritual head of the community; his duties included supervising religious institutions and presiding over the communal court. Other Jewish communal needs were met by *khevres*—associations, subsidiary to the governing board, that ministered to educational, occupational, religious, and social needs. The governing board was the legal representative of the local Jewish community vis-à-vis the Polish authorities and was responsible for collecting state taxes. From about 1580 until 1764, all Jewish communities in Poland were represented and led by a central body—the Council of the Four Lands.

For one hundred and fifty years after the partition, Poland was subject to Austria, Prussia, and Russia. The Jewish communities lost their previous legal status; individuals became directly subject to the state. In Russia and Congress Poland, Jewish self-government, which had gradually been weakened from within, was now restricted by the Czarist authorities, who in 1822–1823 abolished the old governing boards in Congress Poland, replacing them with synagogue boards officially limited to performing religious and social-welfare duties. In Russia, the kehillah lost its legal status in 1844. Jewish communal life was maintained however, primarily by the *khevres*. They were fictitiously registered as private associations, but they assumed many of the functions of the abolished governing boards in addition to their other duties. Although the Czarist authorities deprived the Jewish communities of many powers, they forced them to collect special head taxes and, in the Pale of Settlement, to conscript Jewish recruits for the army, further compromising their communal authority.

After Poland regained her independence in 1918, the Jewish community was officially recognized as a religious as-

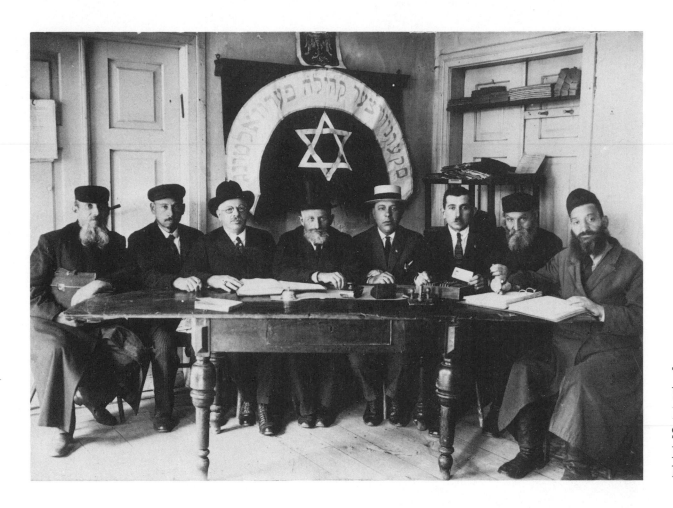

The executive board of the kehillah in Skierniewice. Photographer: L. Karp

Joshua Heschel Farbstein, Zionist leader, member of the Polish Parliament, and chairman of the Warsaw kehillah, lays a wreath on the Tomb of the Unknown Soldier on Polish Independence Day, November 11, 1928. *Nasz Przegląd*, November 18, 1928

Rabbi Leybl Eisenberg, the town rabbi of Łask, in 1938. He died in the Chełmno death camp in 1942.
Photographer: Roman Vishniac

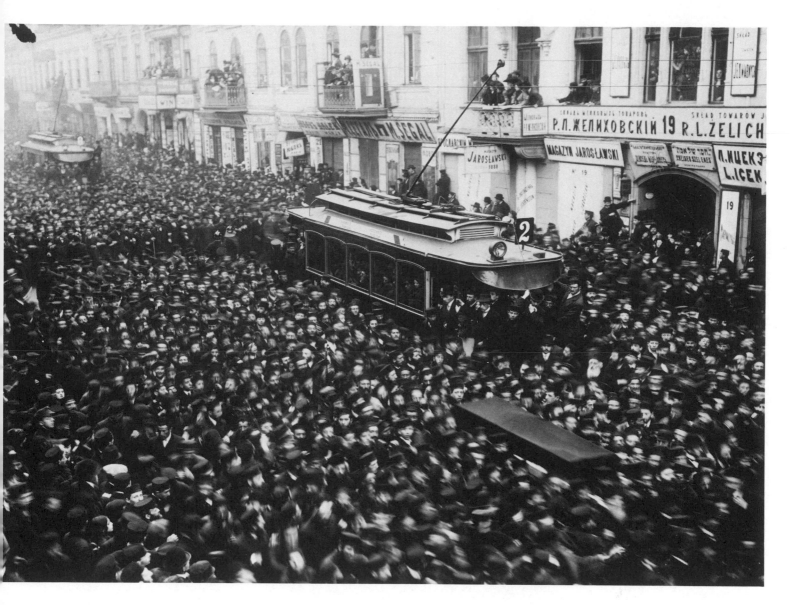

The funeral of Rabbi Elias Haim Meisel (1821–1912) in Łódź. Rabbi Meisel, a great philanthropist, built a factory for handweavers who were unemployed as a result of the mechanization of the textile industry. Studio: American Photographer

sociation in which all Jews were automatically members; it was legally empowered to maintain religious and charitable organizations. The government also recognized a central kehillah, defined as a federation of all individual communities, which was to be supervised by a religious board consisting of seventeen rabbis and thirty-four lay members. This board was never constituted, however, and its duties were performed by the government, which supervised the budgets of local kehillahs and approved the election of officers to their governing boards. As in previous periods, the kehillah continued to maintain synagogues, cemeteries, and Talmud Torahs, and to provide social services by supporting orphanages, hospitals, old-age homes, interest-free loan societies, and relief institutions. In contrast with pre-partitioned Poland, in which the governing board had exercised exclusive control over all aspects of communal life, in independent Poland its authority was limited. Political parties, religious factions, and associations like TOZ, Centos, and ORT, were independent of the kehillah's control and created their own social service institutions.

In the Second Polish Republic the kehillah governing boards and their subsidiary associations thus regained considerable influence since they continued to supervise religious and communal institutions, had the power to certify births, marriages, and deaths (thus to a great extent controlling the legal status of the individual), and distributed funds and administered much of the relief and other social services. During the 1920s, elections were conducted in a more democratic fashion (although the *Agudas yisroel* [Agudath Israel] succeeded in preventing the granting of suffrage to women) and representatives of almost all political and social movements in the community—from *Agudas yisroel* to the Zionist and Socialist parties—vied for positions on the executive board to ensure that their interests were represented. In the 1930s, however, the government sometimes prevented members of the more radical groups from being elected to the kehillah governing board.

The religious character of Jewish self-government and the hegemony that the Orthodox faction, *Agudas yisroel,* continued to exercise were opposed by the other parties. Despite these conflicts the kehillah was a conciliatory force in the community, bringing adversary groups together at a forum in which an effort was made to arrive at a policy for the Jewish community as a whole.

Dvora Esther Gelfer (1817–1907),
philanthropist and founder of a
gmiles khesed society, which provided small, interest-free loans.
Vilna.

Poor boys in Szereszów are
measured for new clothes,
purchased for them by the
kehillah. *Forward* Collection

Jewish Sports Club of Białystok, 1923.

Emergency ambulances in front of the garage of the Jewish *Lines-hatsedek* (First-Aid) association.
Białystok, 1928. Studio: B. Łożnicki

Surgeons attending an international conference in Warsaw visit the operating room of the hospital maintained by the Warsaw kehillah. *Nasz Przegląd,* July 28, 1929

In the garden of the Jewish home for the aged at 17 Portowa Street, Vilna. Photographer: Moryc Grossman/Ephim H. Jeshurin Collection

Passover seder in a Polish military guardhouse, arranged by the Tomhei Asurim (Supporters of the Imprisoned) association, 1927. *Nasz Przegląd* press photograph/Photographer: H. Bojm

Boys and girls in the clubroom and library of an orphanage run by Centos, a Jewish children's-aid society, in Pińsk.

Janusz Korczak (Dr. Henryk Goldszmit), famous writer of children's books and educator, who directed an orphanage in Warsaw for over thirty years. Although he was exempted from the deportation order that sent the children in his orphanage to the death camps, Korczak chose to go with them. From Janusz Korczak, *Wybór Pism*, vol. 2 (Warsaw: Nasza Księgarnia, 1958)

Pupils and teachers of a *kheyder* in Bogorja, 1930. The *kheyder* was supported by the Bogorja Relief Association in Chicago.

TOZ

TOZ—*Towarzystwo Ochrony Zdrowia* (Society for the Safeguarding of Health)—was established in 1921 and was subsidized by the American Joint Distribution Committee and by the OSE *(Oeuvre de Secours aux Enfants)*, an international Jewish health-care organization founded in Russia during the Czarist period. TOZ provided comprehensive health care for Jews throughout Poland.

Visitors at a TOZ summer colony for children in need of fresh air and good food. This colony was named for Cemach Szabad, former chairman of the society, who died in 1935. The guests included the historian Simon Dubnow, the writer Daniel Charney and his wife, and the painter Marc Chagall and his wife.

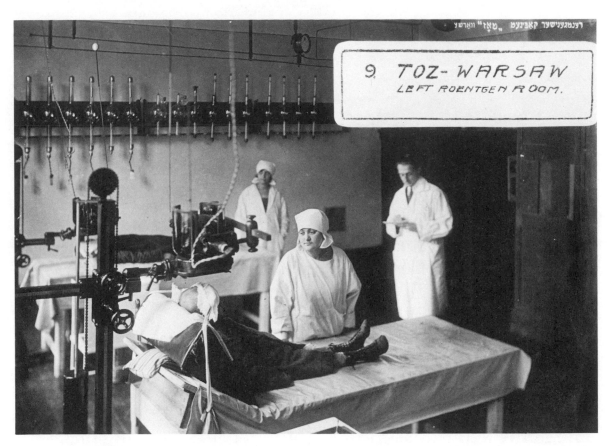

X-ray room in a
TOZ clinic in
Warsaw, post-
World War I. Dr.
Jacob J. Golub
Collection

Children in the TOZ summer colony on the outskirts of Vilna, in the 1930s. Seated
on the ground, the children form the letters of the acronym TOZ in Yiddish.
Ephim H. Jeshurin Collection

SOCIAL AND POLITICAL MOVEMENTS

The Jewish Enlightenment and the emancipation of Jews during the latter half of the nineteenth century gave rise to modern Jewish social and political movements. The Haskalah, which gained its initial influence in Eastern Europe in Galicia and the Pale of Settlement, provided the ideologies of national renewal. Emancipation brought Jews equal rights as citizens, although there continued to be obstacles impeding their full integration into the larger society. Both forces contributed to the decline of the kehillah as the sole form of communal organization. The Jewish intelligentsia, which was most strongly assimilationist in Congress Poland, had tended to enter Polish and Russian movements; but as anti-Semitism intensified, Jewish assimilationism lost ground and involvement in Jewish national and political movements increased.

Jewish political life was shaped in large measure by the minority status, urban concentration, high literacy rate, and occupational structure of the Jewish population. The Jewish proletariat consisted primarily of craftsmen, who worked in small workshops and were heir to a long but waning tradition of workers' associations (in the form of *khevres*); they were among those hardest hit by the deteriorating economic situation. These factors contributed to the involvement of many Jews both in Jewish political parties and in non-Jewish radical movements, which were generally more open to participation by Jews and seemed to offer them greater hope of improving their condition.

Jews of various political persuasions had fought for Polish independence in the hope that it would guarantee their rights as individuals and as a nationality, but in fact the Second Polish Republic failed to live up to the legal provisions of the National Minorities Treaty of 1919 and the Constitution of

1921. The Polish nationalists refused to recognize the multinational character of Poland (ethnic minorities made up one-third of Poland's total population) and intensified their policy of Polonization and their efforts to undermine the rights of the minority groups. The situation deteriorated even further during the thirties, with the decline of democracy and the growth of fascist organizations in Poland. Polish independence, instead of improving the condition of the Jews as they had hoped, had served to intensify anti-Semitism.

However, the Polish parliamentary structure and electoral system, which in principle allowed proportional representation to all ethnic minorities, encouraged a proliferation of political parties. Although over sixty Polish and minority parties were active, and about thirty of these were represented in the Parliament, there were only five major Polish parties. The seven most important Jewish parties grew out of the following movements: traditional Orthodoxy, autonomism, socialism, and Zionism. The assimilationists, rather than form their own Jewish party, entered various Polish ones, including the Social Democratic party of Poland and Lithuania, one of whose founders was Rosa Luxemburg; the Polish Socialist party, among whose leaders were Herman Diamand and Feliks Perl; and the Polish Communist party, one of whose chairmen was Adolf Warski (Warszawski). In the five elections to the Polish Parliament between 1919 and 1938, ninety-seven Jewish deputies and senators were elected as a result of election coalitions of Jewish parties with each other and with various non-Jewish liberal parties.

In 1916, Orthodox Jews established a Polish branch of the *Agudas yisroel* (Agudath Israel) party, which soon became its largest and most active section. The *Agudas yisroel* had been founded as an international movement four years earlier by representatives from Austria-Hungary, Germany, Congress Poland, and the Pale of Settlement. The aim of the *Agudas yisroel* was to preserve the supremacy of rabbinic authority and to protect the Orthodox Jews in Central and Eastern Europe from the influences of Reform Judaism, Zionism, socialism, and assimilation. The *Agudas yisroel* eventually developed its own youth, women's, and labor movements, dominated the kehillah governing board, and was well represented in the municipal councils and in Parliament. It received strong support from the Hasidic sector, especially from the powerful court of *Ger.* Because of its policy of accommodation, the *Agudas yisroel* maintained good relations with the Polish government, which it supported more fully than did other Jewish parties. Orthodox Jews, by organizing a political movement and party, adopted a modern strategy to preserve a traditional lifestyle.

The autonomists established the Jewish Folkist party *(Yidishe folks-partey in poyln)* during World War I. The party grew out of the Eastern European Jewish populist movement which began in Russia at the turn of the century. Its founder was the historian Szymon Dubnow, who formulated the ideology of Jewish autonomism. The Folkists advocated not only cultural autonomy but also political autonomy, which would entail the organization of a Jewish parliament to represent the entire Jewish population of Poland and to figure as a distinct body within the Polish Parliament. Unlike the Zionists and Territorialists (who believed that the place where the Jewish homeland should be established need not necessarily be Palestine), the Folkists believed that Jews did not require their own territory in order to achieve full autonomy. They valued Diaspora culture and supported Yiddish as the Jewish national language. Their constituency consisted of non-Zionist and nonsocialist elements. Initially quite strong, their support dwindled as it became clear that their aims could not be realized.

All Jewish parties came to regard Jews as a national group, demanded a measure of autonomy for them, and provided their followers with a total way of life. Some even formed their own communities, such as the Zionist kibbutzim in Poland. Jewish movements supported their own schools, libraries, newspapers, health-care centers, workers' kitchens, trade unions, cooperative shops, self-defense groups, and cultural organizations—music and theater groups, literary circles, and sports clubs. In this way, they fashioned a modern Jewish culture in line with their particular ideology.

Zionism

Dedicated to the reestablishment of the Jewish state in Palestine and the revival of Hebrew as a national language, the Zionist movement attracted a large following in Eastern Europe, first in Galicia and later in the Pale of Settlement and Congress Poland. Polish Jews were well represented at the

Dr. Zygmunt Bychowski, (1865–1934), a prominent neurologist, communal leader and delegate to the First Zionist Conference in Basle in 1897. Studio: Rembrandt, Warsaw/Marta Osnos Collection

Nachum Sokolow (1859–1936), with his family in Warsaw. Sokolow was a writer and editor for the Hebrew-language newspaper *Hatzefira*. Later he became president of the World Zionist Organization.

historic Lovers of Zion Conference in Katowice, Silesia in 1884, and at all the later world conventions. The Zionist movement in Poland was divided into four major independent parties. The General Zionists attracted the middle class and intelligentsia; of all Jewish parties, the General Zionists had the greatest number of representatives in the Polish Parliament. The Mizrachi was founded in 1902 in Vilna by Orthodox Jews as a branch of the World Mizrachi party. The Poale Zion (Labor Zionists) drew its members from the intelligentsia and lower middle and working classes. The militant Revisionist party was formally constituted in Poland in 1931 by the followers of Vladimir Jabotinsky. The Revisionists believed that the establishment of an independent Jewish state in Palestine could be achieved only by force.

Realizing that emigration to Palestine was a long-range solution, however, the Zionists devoted much of their energy to the immediate condition of Jews in Poland and demanded full civil and political rights and cultural autonomy for them.

David Ben-Gurion (David Grün) on a visit from Palestine, shown with his family in his native town Płońsk, ca. 1910.

Delegates to the national convention of the Mizrachi, the Orthodox Zionist movement. Warsaw, 1916.

Members of the Hashomer Hatzair, a Labor Zionist youth organization. Ostróg, ca. 1921.

Labor Zionists march in a May Day parade. Chełm, 1932.

Vladimir (Zev) Jabotinsky (1880–1940), world leader of the Zionist Revisionist movement and founder of the Jewish Legion in Palestine during World War I. Postcard: Verlag Jehudia, Warsaw

Skiers from the Maccabee Sports Club on the slopes outside Vilna. Ephim H. Jeshurin Collection

The first motorcycle team of the Warsaw Maccabee. *Nasz Przegląd*, November 17, 1929

Members of the stonecutters' kibbutz at work. Klesów, 1930s.

Jews leaving for Palestine. New Year's greeting card. Postcard: Verlag
S. Resnik, Warsaw and New York

Wilhelm Ryppel, leader of the "Liberation March to Palestine," an attempt by Zionist youth to defy the British ban on immigration. Warsaw, 1930s. *Der tog* Collection

Socialism

The Bund—*Algemeyner yidisher arbeter bund in lite, poyln, un rusland* (the General Jewish Workers Alliance of Lithuania, Poland, and Russia)—was founded secretly in 1897 in Vilna. Originally intended to draw Jewish workers into the Russian socialist movement, the Bund was at various times a section of the Russian Social Democratic party. Unable to resolve conflicts with the Russian party, however, and aware that Jewish workers faced problems of a special character, the Bund eventually established itself as a separate Jewish socialist movement.

The Bund's ultimate goal was to create a socialist society, but its immediate concerns were with workers' rights in general and with Jewish needs in particular—full national and cultural autonomy, civil and political rights, and the establishment of Yiddish as the Jewish national language. Subsidiary organizations of the Bund were devoted specifically to women

The Bund was founded in this house in Vilna in 1897. Photographer: Moryc Grossman

Vladimir Medem (1879–1923), writer and leader of the Bund.

Student member of the Bund. Świsłocz, 1908. Photographer: A. Kacev, Taurogen

(YAF—*Yidishe arbeter froyen*), children (SKIF—*Sotsyalistisher kinder farband*), youth *(Tsukunft)*, and to the many kinds of cultural activities necessary for the development of a modern secular Jewish society. The Bund, which in general refused to enter a coalition with bourgeois parties, failed to win any seats in the Polish Parliament; however, it was very well represented and powerful in the municipal councils and kehillah governing boards, especially in the late 1930s. One of its most important contributions was the organization of labor unions.

Playground at the sanatorium named in honor of Vladimir Medem. Miedzeszyn, near Warsaw, 1930s. Originally a tubercular children's sanatorium, it later provided health care and education for other children as well. Between 1925, when it was founded, and 1939, more than 10,000 children were cared for here.

Henokh Goldschmidt, a Bundist, reading the Bund party newspaper *Folkstsaytung*. Gąbin, 1925. J. M. Rothbart Collection

Members of the Bund youth organization on a climbing expedition in the Tatry mountains, led by Borys Eisurowicz, a pedagogue who organized mountain-climbing expeditions for Jewish workers. Bund Archives of the Jewish Labor Movement, New York

Yosef Lipszyc, a Bund leader and
organizer of the transport workers,
with a driver. Warsaw, 1938.
Photographer: Roman Vishniac

May Day 1933 in Warsaw. Henryk Erlich speaks at the close of the Bund demonstration in front of the party club on Przejazd Street. Bund Archives of the
Jewish Labor Movement, New York

EDUCATION

During the nineteenth century, the traditional educational institutions, *kheyder* and yeshivah, came under severe attack. Efforts were made to undermine their influence both by *maskilim* (adherents of the Haskalah) and by the Russian authorities. In 1813, Joseph Perl, a *maskil*, established a private school in Tarnopol, one of the first to combine Jewish and secular studies. Similar efforts were made in other cities, although the number of students was very small. Jewish enrollment in government schools was also very limited. Many Jews were opposed to secular education. Others were dissuaded from attending the state schools because of their Christian character and the abuse suffered by Jewish students.

During the 1840s, in order to promote assimilation, the Russian government invited Max Lilienthal, a rabbi and pedagogue from Germany, to establish, in the Pale of Settlement, modern government-controlled schools especially for Jews. Most of the Jewish population opposed Lilienthal's efforts. In the following decades, the government proceeded to establish about one hundred state schools for Jews, which were very poorly attended at first. During the last decades of the nineteenth century—with legal emancipation, liberalized government education policies, and the growing impact of progressive movements within the Jewish community—Jews began to enter regular government schools, where in 1881 they constituted 12.3 percent of the students, and to enroll in the universities in increasing numbers.

Many Jewish intellectuals saw educational reform as essential to the modernization of Jewish life and the entry of Jews into the larger society. By the end of the nineteenth century, however, most were disillusioned with their futile attempts to enter this society and they began instead to be caught up in the growing tide of Jewish nationalism.

Some gave their support to Zionism and the revival of Hebrew as a national language. As a result, new types of

Boys entering the Mefitzah Haskalah school in Vilna, 1929. Mefitzah Haskalah (Disseminators of Enlightenment) established teacher-training courses and boys' and girls' schools in which courses in modern Hebrew and Jewish history were offered. Ephim H. Jeshurin Collection

secular Jewish schools were developed—examples are the *heder metukkan*, or "improved *kheyder*," and the Zionist-sponsored Tarbut schools. The "improved *kheyder*" was informed by modern pedagogical ideas—"Hebrew taught in Hebrew," for example—and their kindergarten teachers attended Froebel courses. The Tarbut schools were secular in orientation, used Hebrew as the language of instruction, instilled the ideals of Zionism in the young, and sought to prepare them for a life in Palestine. In 1922, the Tarbut was legally constituted as a central school organization.

At the Chernevtsy Yiddish Language Conference in 1908, Yiddish was also recognized as a national language. Like Hebrew, Yiddish became ideologically central to new social and political movements and to the creation of a modern school

Mandolin orchestra of the I. L. Peretz School, a secular Yiddish primary school, in Białystok, 1924. Photographer: B. Polski

system. CYSHO—*Tsentrale yidishe shul-organizatsye* (Central Jewish School Organization)—was founded in 1921, although the first secular Yiddish school had been established illegally more than twenty years earlier. The CYSHO schools were secular, used Yiddish as the language of instruction, and were supported by Jewish socialist parties.

Polish-Hebrew bilingual schools were first established in 1912 as a response to the limited access Jews had to state schools. These schools, whose central body was the Federation of Jewish Secondary Schools, served middle-class Jews who valued Polish acculturation, but wished to preserve their Jewish national identification, and who were committed to the Zionist cause.

SHULKULT—*Shul un kultur farband* (Federation for School and Culture)—which was supported by the Labor Zionists and others, placed equal emphasis on Yiddish and Hebrew as languages of instruction. The state requirement that Polish be used to teach Polish subjects made these schools trilingual.

Schoolboys playing chess at the Yehudit summer colony for Orthodox boys. Długosiodło, 1930s. Studio: Forbert/Raphael Abramovitch Collection

Like the other political parties, the *Agudas yisroel* developed its own modern school network, and consistent with traditional ultraorthodox education, religious study was central to its curriculum. Boys attended the Horev schools and girls the Beth Jacob schools, which were founded by Sarah Schenirer in Cracow in 1917. In addition, the *Agudas yisroel* supported yeshivahs, some of which achieved international reputations, as well as teacher-training institutes. The Orthodox Zionists (Mizrachi) supported their own religious schools, the Yavneh schools.

The importance of education to the realization of national ideals and the failure of the government to live up to the stipulations of the national-minorities clauses of the Versailles Treaty of 1919 made it necessary for the Jewish community in Poland and abroad to bear the financial responsibility for Jewish schools in Poland. The Treaty stated that the Polish government was to provide, within the public educational system, primary school instruction for national minorities in their own language and to allocate public funds for minority-group education. The government supported its own Polish-oriented *Szabasówka* schools for Jews but failed to establish Hebrew and Yiddish primary schools or to subsidize adequately those that the Jewish community organized. The Treaty also stipulated that the national minorities of Poland had the right to establish and control their own institutions of learning at their own expense and to use their own language and practice their religion in these schools. In the 1920s, in order to secure legal recognition from the government, Jewish elementary schools had to offer a minimum of ten to twelve hours a week of instruction in Polish on Polish subjects. Most Jewish secondary schools did not receive accreditation and their graduates were therefore not admitted to Polish universities. The state board of education, which exercised control over all private schools, could prevent schools from opening and could close them down, and in the 1930s, repressive government action forced some schools to close.

Children and staff of a kindergarten, 1911. Studio: Murillon

Here rests our fly." Vilna, 1927. Kinder-
arten children at the grave of their fly.
phim H. Jeshurin Collection

Homeless boys, cared for by a Jewish educational association.
Vilna, 1936. Ephim H. Jeshurin Collection

choolboys doing gymnastics, Vilna. Studio: Bracia Bietkowscy

Children in Purim costume, at the S. M. Gurewicz high school in Vilna, 1933.

TRADE SCHOOLS

The Jewish community responded to discriminatory practices in state-owned trade schools by creating vocational schools to train Jews for industry, agriculture, crafts, commerce, administration, communication, and surveying. As early as 1888, Baron de Hirsch had provided funds for establishing trade schools in Galicia and Bukovina; these were the first schools outside Palestine to introduce modern Hebrew instruction. Jewish trade schools were maintained by local communities with the help of the AJDC (American Joint Distribution Committee), ORT (Organization for Rehabilitation through Training), WUZET (Organization for Professional Education, Galicia), JCA (Jewish Colonization Association), and other philanthropic organizations.

The laboratory of a trade school for girls. Studio: Marion/*Der tog* Collection

Exhibit at a trade school for seamstresses. Pińsk, 1936.

KURS KROJU MĘSKIEGO i DAMSKIEGO URZĄDZONY STARANIEM ZW RZEMIŚL RZEGZ. POLSKIEL
ODDZIAŁ w TARNOWIE POD KIER. P. PROF. G. PAPIERA z WARSZAWY.

Professor G. Papier of Warsaw conducts a class in fashion design for tailors. Tarnów, 1928.

Homemaking class—to train Jewish women to be professional housekeepers— sponsored by the Women's Aid Organization. Vilna, 1938. The two signs, in Yiddish, distinguish between utensils for meat products and those for dairy products.

Display of model furniture in an ORT trade school. Warsaw, 1920s. The base of the table is shaped like a menorah. Photographer: J. Malarski

School of Nursing, Jewish Hospital in Warsaw, 1939.

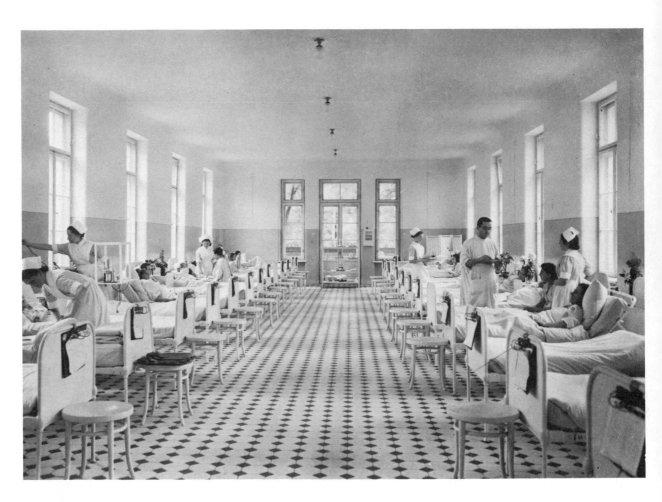

Surgical
ward

Visiting
nurses

Main hall of the student residence

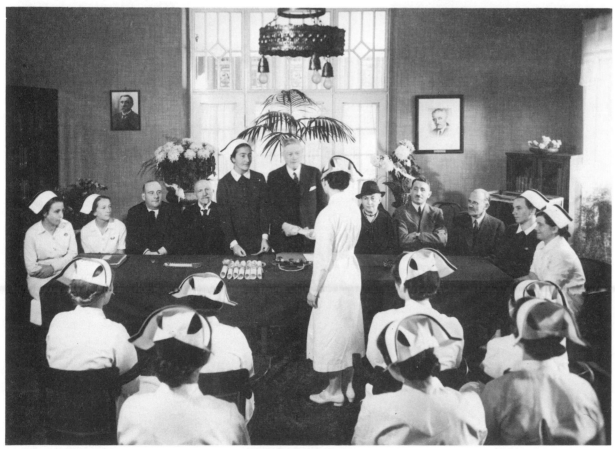

Award of diplomas

SCHOLARSHIP

Until the late nineteenth century, the only institutions of Jewish learning in Poland were yeshivahs and Talmudic academies. Secular studies, mainly in philosophy, astronomy, and philology, were pursued individually by rabbis and laymen. The first liberal profession to which the Polish Jews gained entry was medicine. Since Polish universities were closed to them, Jewish physicians either were self-taught or received their educations abroad, in Spain at first and later in Italy.

The turning point in the development of secular learning among the Jews came with their legal emancipation in the second half of the nineteenth century, when the prohibition on Jewish attendance at Polish high schools and universities was removed. Jewish scholars did not readily obtain teaching positions in the universities, however, and many worked independently or in research institutes. There were Jewish scholars in many fields, especially mathematics and physics, economics, demography, statistics, history, and literature. In the 1930s, restrictions were again imposed on the admission of Jews to the universities, and the percentage of Jewish students fell from a high of about twenty percent to fifteen percent.

The first secular Jewish academic institutions were established late in the nineteenth century, but Jewish intellectual life

1   Chaim Zelig Słonimski (1810-1904), founder of *Hatzefira*, a Hebrew-language newspaper devoted mainly to scientific topics. He was also a mathematician and astronomer, improved the calculating machine invented by his son-in-law, Abraham Stern, and was responsible for improvements in the steam engine and telegraph. Postcard: Lebanon Society

2   Ludwik Zamenhof (1857-1917), philologist and creator of Esperanto. The Royal Library of Copenhagen Collection

3   The Lublin Yeshivah. Founded in 1930 by Rabbi Majer Szapira, it was one of the most distinguished modern Talmudic academies in the Diaspora. From Hilel Seidman, *Szlakiem nauki talmudycznej* (Warsaw: F. Hoesick, 1934)

1

2

3

Jacob Shatzky (1893–1956), Jewish historian and author of a three-volume history of the Jews of Warsaw. Warsaw, 1914. He is pictured in the uniform of the Polish Legions, in which he served before emigrating to America in 1922.

Emmanuel Ringelblum (1900–1944), historian. He established an underground research institute and archives in the Warsaw Ghetto. His archives, recovered after the war, constitute a basic source on the Holocaust and the Jewish resistance movement in the Warsaw Ghetto.

Dr. Mark Dworzecki and other members of the Art and History Lovers of Cracow Antiquities visit the Wawel Royal Castle in Cracow in 1937.

was able to develop fully only after World War I in independent Poland. During the years 1918–1939, the most important Jewish scholarly institutions were:

1. The YIVO Institute for Jewish Research, *founded in Vilna in 1925. YIVO devoted itself to research on all aspects of East European Jewish culture. Among its most prominent scholars were S. Dubnow, M. Weinreich, E. Tcherikower, and Z. Reisen.*
2. The Institute for Jewish Studies, *in Warsaw, under the leadership of M. Schorr, M. Bałaban, and A. Weiss. It included departments of biblical and Talmudic studies, philosophy of religion, Hebrew literature, and classical studies, in addition to sociology, demography, and statistics.*
3. Takhemoni, *an institute established by the Mizrachi movement to provide secular as well as religious higher education for rabbis.*

Committee of the YIVO, in front of their half-completed building. Vilna, 1929. From left to right: B. Wirgili-Kahan, J. Zheleznikov, Z. H. Kalmanowicz, (unidentified), M. Weinreich, I. N. Steinberg, C. Zhitlowsky, J. Szapiro, Z. Reisen, M. Czernichow, and B. Kleckin.

4

Each of the Jewish scholarly institutions had its own library and archives. Some libraries functioned independently—one of the most prominent was the Strashun rabbinical library, established in Vilna in 1892. Many institutions published their own periodicals and books in many languages and maintained close relations with world Jewish centers of learning, especially in Palestine and the United States.

1 Institute for Jewish Studies on Tłomackie Street in Warsaw, late 1930s. Photographer: C. Najberg

2 Majer Bałaban (1877–1942), historian, professor at Warsaw University, and for several years head of the Institute for Jewish Studies. Warsaw, 1930s. Studio: Rembrandt/*Forward* Collection

3 Ignacy Schiper (1884–1943), historian, Zionist, and member of the Polish Parliament, at a YIVO conference. Vilna, 1929. Photographer: Alter Kacyzne/Raphael Abramovitch Collection

4 Reading room of the Strashun Library, housed in the Vilna synagogue complex and founded by Mathias Strashun (1819–1885). Vilna, 1939.

WRITERS,
MUSICIANS,
ARTISTS

For centuries, Hebrew was the medium for a prolific rabbinic literature and Yiddish the vehicle for a popular literature— translations of the Bible and Aggadah, epics and romances, and chapbooks of legends of saints and traditional tales. Toward the end of the eighteenth century, with the rise and spread of Hasidism and the Haskalah, Hebrew and Yiddish were gradually forged into modern literary languages, and a thriving modern literature in each began to develop.

The Hebrew Haskalah in Western Europe made its first inroads in Poland in Galicia in the first decades of the nineteenth century. It was in this area, where Hasidism had arisen and claimed its firmest hold, that Hasidic literary and cultural activity later flourished. Early exponents of the Hebrew Haskalah in Galicia directed their literary efforts into a virulent campaign against Hasidism.

From Galicia, the Haskalah moved to Lithuania and Volhynia. In the north, it stimulated Hebrew and Yiddish literary activity in Vilna and Kovno. Major Hebrew figures writing there were the novelist A. Mapu and the poets M. J. Lebensohn (Adam haKohen), his son Mikhal, and J. L. Gordon. Important Yiddish writers from the 1850s on were Isaac Meir Dick, Jacob Dineson, and N. M. Shaikewitz (Shomer), pioneers of the Yiddish sentimental novel and novelette. In contrast, in Warsaw, where Jewish intellectuals had tended towards Polonization and assimilation, the first neo-Orthodox school of Jewish writing arose. These writers—A. B. Ruf, G. Beloy, and others—used modern Yiddish to create anti-Haskalah fiction and poetry.

During the nineteenth century, the Yiddish literary scene was dominated by writers in the Ukraine and Russia, for example, Mendele Moykher Sforim and Sholom Aleichem. In

1

2

1 Mendele Moykher Sforim (1835–1917), with Jacob Dineson (*to right of Sforim*) and
David Frischmann (*left*), on a visit in 1909 to the Jarosinski trade school in Łódź.
Mendele (pseudonym of S. Abramovitsh) was the ''grandfather'' of modern Yiddish
literature. He headed a literary circle in Odessa. David Frischmann (1860–1922) was
editor of several Hebrew newspapers, translated European literature into Hebrew,
and wrote short stories and poetry.

2 On the left: Mordkhe Spektor (1858–1925), with Sholom Aleichem (pseudonym
of Shalom Rabinowitz). Spektor, a popular Yiddish writer and editor, encouraged
Sholom Aleichem (1859–1916) to write in Yiddish, which was then gaining recognition as a modern literary language. He had previously written in Hebrew and
Russian.

1 Borys Kleckin (1875–1937), publisher and patron of Yiddish literature, with Jacob Dineson (1856–1919), a Yiddish writer whose forte was the sentimental novel. Vilna, 1913. Dineson played an important role in the development of Jewish secular education.

2 S. An-ski (1863–1920) and Samuel Niger (1883–1955). Vilna, ca. 1919. An-ski (pseudonym of Solomon Zainwil Rapaport) is best known for *The Dybbuk*, a play based on a Hasidic legend he recorded during the ethnographic expedition he led between 1911 and 1914. Samuel Niger (pseudonym of Samuel Charney) was a Yiddish literary critic and editor. In 1920, he came to America, where for thirty-five years he contributed to the New York Yiddish daily *Der tog*. Studio: Broudner

3 Isaac Leib Peretz (1852–1915), master of modern Yiddish literature, Yiddish and Hebrew poet, dramatist, and short-story writer. Peretz was famous for his neoromantic and symbolist style. Publisher: Verlag Jehudia, Warsaw

2

3

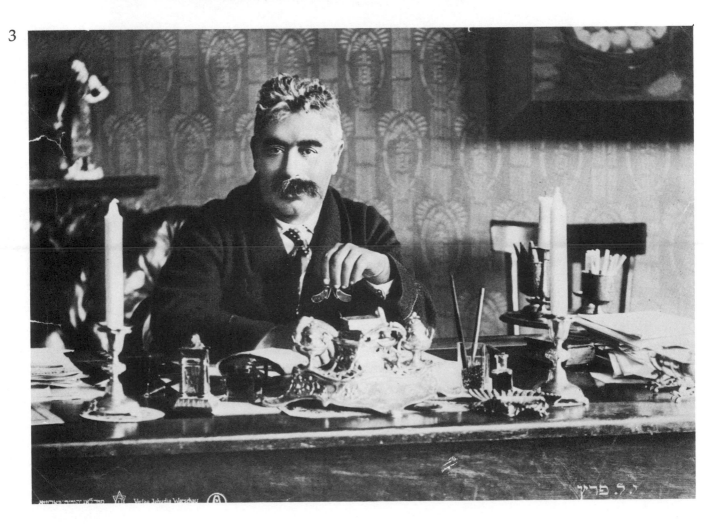

Sholem Asch, Isaac Leib Peretz, Peretz's son Lucjan (left to right), and Hersh Dovid Nomberg (1876–1927). Nomberg lies on the grass. Nomberg, a Yiddish and Hebrew essayist and short-story writer, was a founder of the *Folkist* Party and a member of the Polish Parliament.

Der Tunkeler (J. Tunkel, 1881–1949), Yiddish humorist and cartoonist, Mordkhe Spektor, and Jeushson (Moshe Bunem Justman, 1889–1942), Yiddish journalist and novelist.

Judah Leib Gordon (1831–1892), vitriolic Hebrew journalist and poet of the Haskalah. Elias Tcherikower Collection

Abraham Reisen (1876–1953), Yiddish poet and short-story writer. A disciple of Peretz, in 1914 Reisen came to New York, where he wrote for the American Yiddish press.

the twentieth century, Poland became the major center of activity. The shift was precipitated by the meteoric rise of I. L. Peretz as a Yiddish and Hebrew writer. Peretz became the living symbol of Jewish literary and intellectual life in Poland.

Warsaw was one of the two major centers of Hebrew literary activity in Eastern Europe from 1880 to 1914, the other center being Odessa. Most Hebrew periodicals and publishing houses were concentrated in Warsaw, where such influential writers as David Frischmann and Nachum Sokolow worked. As a result, Warsaw became the locus of all young Hebrew writers at the turn of the century. By the end of World War I, Hebrew had shifted its center to Palestine and found itself on the wane in Poland. However, Hebrew literary activity did continue in Poland up until and even during the Holocaust, particularly around the great literary salon of the poet and dramatist Yitskhak Katzenelson in Łódź, in the playwriting of M. M. Shoham, and in the poetry of Berl Pomerantz.

Warsaw was also the focal point of Yiddish writing in Poland, which had crystallized around the leadership of I. L. Peretz. (He had made his debut in Yiddish in 1888, having first written in Polish and Hebrew.) In contrast with the intense anti-Hasidic writing of so many nineteenth-century literary figures, Peretz initiated a neo-Hasidic trend by making the hagiography and mystical tales of the Hasidim the basis for a significant part of his work. Peretz attracted a coterie of gifted writers.

During the interwar years, various literary circles arose in Warsaw, all of them claiming Peretz as their legacy. Among the Realists, or Naturalists, as they were called, were Isaac Meir Weissenberg, who treated conflict and change in Jewish life in small towns, and Oyzer Warszawski, who made his reputation with *Shmuglars* (1920), a novel about the Jewish underworld during the German occupation of World War I. The Idealists included symbolist poets, the dramatist Alter Kacyzne, and the novelist I. I. Trunk. *Di khalyastre* (The Gang) introduced into Yiddish poetry expressionism and other modernist trends encountered in Russian and German poetry.

Innovative Yiddish poetry was also being written in Łódź and in Lwów, the center of Yiddish literary activity in Galicia. Moshe Broderson played an important role in transmitting to Łódź the modernist ideas developing in Warsaw. In Lwów, such neo-romantic poets as Mendl Neugroeshel, Samuel Jacob Imber, and Melekh Ravitch were strongly influenced by German symbolist poets, especially Rainer Marie Rilke.

Vilna came to the fore as a Yiddish literary center with the emergence of Moshe Kulbak in the 1920s and the formation of *Yung vilne* (Young Vilna) in the 1930s. Moshe Kulbak reacted against the neo-romanticism of I. L. Peretz and against a proliferating popular literature, which included the old-school sentimental poetry of David Einhorn and Zusman Segalowitch and sub-rosa pulp novels, detective thrillers, and erotic romances. Kulbak, who left Vilna for the Soviet Union in 1928, served as the literary model for *Yung vilne*. Ideologically committed to socialism, *Yung vilne* was somewhat more traditional in its approach to form than the modernist poets in Warsaw. Among its distinguished members were the poet Avrom Sutzkever, living today in Israel, and the poet and novelist Chaim Grade, who now resides in New York City.

Standing, to the right: Joseph Opatoshu (1886–1954), on a visit from America in 1924, with his family. Opatoshu emigrated in 1907; he was one of the first to treat the American Jewish experience in a Yiddish literary work.

Mendl Elkin, Peretz Hirschbein, Uri Zvi Greenberg, Peretz Markish, Melekh Ravitch, and Israel Joshua Singer in Warsaw, 1922. They called themselves *Di khalyastre* ("The Gang"). Markish and Singer edited the *Khalyastre almanakh*, a Yiddish expressionist literary journal.

Isaac Bashevis Singer (*right*) and his brother Israel Joshua Singer (d. 1944), distinguished Yiddish novelists. I. J. Singer is noted for his symbolist dramas and epic "family" novels. I. B. Singer came to America in 1935. Many of his works have been translated into English.

Jews also wrote in the coterritorial literary languages, especially Polish in the central provinces, Russian in the northeast, and German in the southwest. Indeed, during the nineteenth century, most Jewish writers began their careers in one of these languages or in Hebrew before turning their hand to Yiddish. In the twentieth century, the literary creativity of Jews writing in Polish reached its peak in the work of the poets and novelists Julian Tuwim, Bruno Schulz, and Józef Wittlin.

Julian Tuwim (1894–1953). He wrote in the Polish language and was Poland's greatest modern poet.

Bruno Schulz (1892–1942). His expressionist and surrealist tales are among the finest in Polish literature. Dr. Joseph Sperling Collection

Józef Wittlin (1896–1976) and his wife Halina on their honeymoon. Lwów, 1924.
He was one of Poland's most distinguished novelists and poets.

Roman Kramsztyk
(1885–1942), a dis-
tinguished painter,
photographed in
his studio.

Artur Rubinstein, pianist.

THEATER

Yiddish folk drama was for centuries the only kind of theater performed by Polish Jews. By the 1830s the first modern Yiddish plays were being read by amateur drama circles in Warsaw and Cracow. Later, in the 1880s, the growth of professional Yiddish theater in Poland received a major stimulus from the activities of the prolific playwright and producer Abraham Goldfaden. In 1883, in areas of Poland under Czarist rule, Yiddish theater per se was banned—in order to exist at all it was forced to call itself "German-Yiddish" theater. In

Abraham Goldfaden (1840–1908), father of the Yiddish theater, playwright, director, and composer.

Esther Rokhl Kamińska (1870–1925). She pioneered in the development of the Yiddish art theater and acted in the first Jewish films, which were made in Warsaw at the turn of the century. Photographer: J. Ejgel

Austria-Hungary, however, Yaakov Ber Gimpel was given the first permit to establish a stable Yiddish theater, in 1888. It remained active in Lwów (Galicia) until World War II.

Until the 1890s, musical comedies, melodramas, and other forms of popular theater dominated the Yiddish repertory. The first amateur art theater group in Poland consisted of a group of self-educated weavers in Łódź who performed from the literary dramatic repertory the works of playwrights such as Peretz and Sholom Aleichem. Around 1900 Avrom Yitskhok

Kamiński and his wife, Esther Rokhl, established a touring ensemble. From 1905 to 1910, during which time the Czarist ban was lifted, the Yiddish theater grew. By 1910 there were about three hundred and sixty amateur theater clubs, some of whose members later became professionals. These clubs were often associated with social or political organizations or with schools. The first professional Yiddish art theater (1908–1910) was established by Peretz Hirschbein in Odessa; it also performed in Warsaw.

Posters, mounted on a horse-drawn cart, advertise the Yiddish theater in Warsaw before World War I. The posters are printed in Polish and Russian.

The Yitskhok Zandberg Company in Łódź, 1910. From 1905 to 1914, Zandberg was director of the Grand Theater in Łódź, where his ensemble performed. He was instrumental in organizing a Yiddish actors' union.

Yiddish theater flourished in Poland during the time of the German occupation (World War I). In 1916, a semi-professional group known as the Organization of Yiddish Actors (FADA) established themselves as the Vilna Troupe. Influenced by Stanislavski's Moscow Art Theater, they became famous for their avant-garde productions of Yiddish and European theater classics. Eight years later, when they were to tour America, the Vilna Troupe split into several smaller companies. In 1923–1924, Zygmunt Turkow and his wife, Ida

Kamińska, named their ensemble the Warsaw Yiddish Art Theater (VYKT—*Varshever yidisher kunst-teater*) and until the outbreak of World War II produced European classics in Yiddish translation and plays written in Yiddish. In addition there were *kleynkunst* theaters, which specialized in satirical and musical revues, Clara Segalovich's popular Theater for Youth (founded in 1926), and local marionette theaters. During the early 1930s, an acting collective of graduates of Michał Weichert's Cultural League Drama Studio, a Yiddish theater school, formed the *Yung teater* (Young Theater), which had an experimental and politically radical orientation. Their first production, *Boston* (1933), was about the Sacco and Vanzetti trial. It was performed more than two hundred times in Warsaw alone.

Producer Leib Kadison (*second row on right*), director Mordecai Mazo (*top row, second from right*), and Noakh Nachbusz (*first row, second from left*), founders of the Vilna Troupe, with members of the ensemble. Vilna, 1916. Studio: Broudner

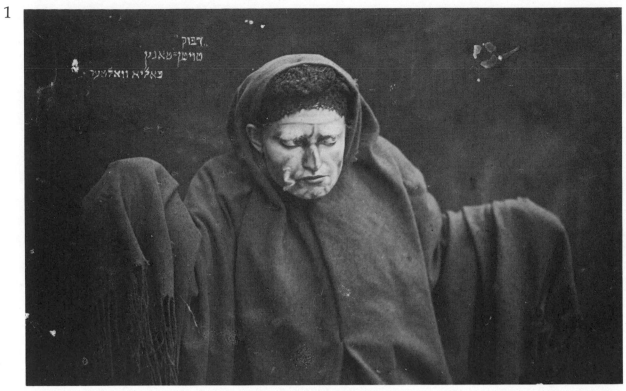

Irma Gowinska as Leah and Zvi Friedland as Khonen, in the Habimah production of *The Dybbuk*. Habimah first produced *The Dybbuk*, in Hebrew, in 1922. Chaim Nachman Bialik was the translator.

1 Paula Walter in the death-dance scene from the Vilna Troupe production of S. An-ski's *The Dybbuk*. First performed by the Vilna Troupe in 1920, *The Dybbuk* made theater history. David Herman's expressionist treatment was the model of hundreds of other productions of the play—in Polish, German, Ukrainian, English, Swedish, Bulgarian, and Hebrew. The play was written in Russian and translated by the author into Yiddish.

2 Lidia Potocka as Mrs. Alving and Khevel Buzgan as Oswald in the final scene of the Vilna Troupe production of Ibsen's *Ghosts*, a favorite play in the Yiddish repertory.

Ida Kamińska as Esmeralda in a Yiddish stage adaptation of Victor Hugo's *Hunchback of Notre Dame,* a VYKT production directed by Zygmunt Turkow. It had its premiere in Vilna in 1925.

Khane Grosberg in a satirical musical revue presented by *Di yidishe bande* ("The Jewish Gang"). Known also as The Bandits, this ensemble was one of the many *kleynkunst* theaters that were popular in Warsaw during the interwar years. In 1939, Khane Grosberg and other members of the ensemble performed in New York. She and some other performers did not return to Poland and thus escaped the war. Studio: Forbert

Szymon Dzigan (*left*) and Shmulik Goldstein (*in carriage*) in a satirical revue presented at the Ararat *kleynkunst* theater in Łódź. Moshe Broderson wrote much of their material. Studio: Polonia

Yiddish theater had its most creative period during the 1920s and 1930s. It had developed a mass audience, a cadre of theater professionals, and its own basic repertory of dramatic classics. In addition it drew upon the plays and stage techniques of European theater, including those of the avant-garde theater. During the 1930s, there were twenty Yiddish companies active in Poland—fifteen companies performed in Vilna alone in 1935.

Although they did not attract as large an audience, there were also amateur Hebrew theater clubs in Poland. The professional Hebrew company Habimah, founded in Moscow in 1917, toured Poland and other countries. Of the approximately seventy-five plays in its repertory before World War II, the most popular play was *The Dybbuk*, which it performed eight

Joseph Buloff, Eliohu Shteyn, and Jacob Waislitz in Sholem Asch's *Amnon and Tamar*, performed by the Vilna Troupe and directed by Mendl Elkin. Warsaw, 1921. Photographer: Alter Kacyzne

Zygmunt Turkow (1896–1970) in Molière's *The Miser*. Warsaw, 1923. *The Miser* was among the most successful productions of the VYKT theater ensemble.

The Vilna Operetta Troupe, in the musical comedy *Kavkazer libe* ("Caucasian Love"). Vilna, 1927. This traveling company was founded in 1926 by Yosef Khash, his wife Nekhome, and his brother Kadish.

hundred and ninety-six times during the first twenty-eight years of its existence. Other favorites were Leivik's *The Golem* and Pinski's *The Quintessential Jew.*

Jews were also active in the Polish theater. They attended Polish drama academies and performed in Polish productions. Polish directors and designers sometimes worked on Jewish theater productions. Many Yiddish plays were translated into Polish and other languages, thereby reaching an international audience.

CINEMA

The first film on a subject of Jewish interest that was seen by Jewish audiences in the Russian empire was a re-creation of the Dreyfus case. Filmed by Francis Doublier of the French Lumière factory, it was shown in the southern provinces of the empire in 1898. Genuine documentaries on the pogroms in Kiev and Kishinev were produced in 1911 by foreign (mostly American) companies and were distributed abroad. Pathé and other foreign companies were also making fictional films about Jews in Russia and Poland. The actors in these films were usually not Jews, but the films made use of a few Jewish "types" for effect. The first movies on Jewish subjects that actually featured Jewish actors were made in Warsaw, the center of the film industry in Congress Poland (although, before World War I, ninety percent of the film industry in the Russian empire was located in Moscow). These movies were performed in Yiddish and were often film versions of Yiddish

In an imaginary cinema, spectators view the arrival of the New Year. New Year's greeting card. Postcard: Verlag S. Resnik, Warsaw and New York

plays and novels. (Of the 2,016 fictional films made in pre-revolutionary Russia, sixty-nine dealt with Jewish subjects and about half of these were adaptations of Yiddish plays or novels.)

Like most producers in the early film industry in the Russian empire, producers of Yiddish films followed the vogue for filming plays which had been established by Le Film d'Art, a company founded in Paris in 1908. Yiddish plays were often filmed in the theaters in which they were being performed to live audiences. In 1912, for example, during its run at the Vilna Circus Theater, *Khasye di yesoyme* ("Khasye the Orphan") was filmed by N. Lipowski during the day, when the theater was empty. The filming took two weeks. Productions were sometimes transported to film studios, where they were mounted and filmed exactly as they had been staged. Film versions of plays by Jacob Gordin, E. Waksman, and others were made by the first Yiddish film companies in Congress Poland—*Siła* and *Variag* (established in Warsaw by two women—Yelizariants and Stern) and *Kosmofilm*. Libin's *Der vilder foter* ("The Wild Father") and Gordin's *Mirele efros* were produced by Mojżesz Mordka Towbin for Siła in 1911 and 1912, and Gordin's *Di shtifmuter* ("The Stepmother") was made by Kosmofilm in 1913. A. I. Kamiński directed and Esther Rokhl Kamińska and other members of their family acted in many of the most popular of the Jewish films made before World War I.

During the twenties and thirties, the film industry in Poland gained momentum. Sfinks, one of the first and largest film companies in Congress Poland, was founded in 1910 by the Jewish producer Aleksander Hertz. He made about half of the two thousand short and feature-length films that were produced in Poland prior to World War II. Most of the films were directed at a general audience, but at least one had a Jewish theme; it was based on a story by Eliza Orzeszkowa. Many of the films on Jewish subjects were considered to be of higher quality than the popular melodramatic Yiddish films that were being made in America and distributed in Poland. Indeed Yiddish films from Poland were very popular in America. Leo

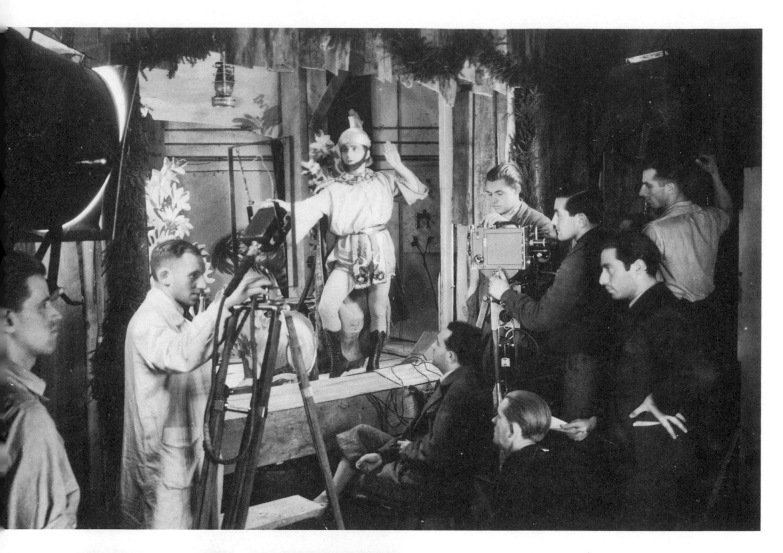

Shooting the film *Freylekhe kabtsonim* ("Happy Paupers"), based on a story by Moshe Broderson and starring Zygmunt Turkow, his daughter Ruth Turkow, Szymon Dzigan, and Yisroel Szumacher.

Jewish youngster studying the Polish cinema magazine *Kino*. Niemenczyn, 1930. Wilhelm Begell Collection

Scene from the film *Poylishe velder* ("Polish Woods"), based on Joseph Opatoshu's novel. It was directed by Jonas Turkow in 1929. A Forbert Company production.

Jonas Turkow directing a scene from the film *Poylishe velder.*

Rokhl Holtser and Khevel Buzgan in *Al-khet* ("Confession"), an early Yiddish sound film directed by Aleksander Marten. A Sektor Company production.

Forbert, a photographer who became a filmmaker, and Henryk Bojm, a scenario writer, made movies on Jewish folk themes—for example, *Tkies-kaf* ("The Vow") in 1923 and *Der lamedvovnik* ("The Secret Saint") in 1925. Three years later Forbert made *Poylishe velder* ("Polish Woods"), based on the novel by Joseph Opatoshu and directed by Jonas Turkow. The cast included non-Jewish as well as Jewish actors. In contrast to the filmed versions of Yiddish plays, *Poylishe velder* was shot on location. The first Yiddish sound film made in Poland, *Al-khet* ("Confession"), was released in 1936 by the Kinor Company. During the same year, a Polish-language documentary made by a radical group *(Start)* was banned from general circulation by the government. Directed by Aleksander Ford, it was about the Medem children's sanatorium of the Bund. The film was known in Jewish circles as *Mir kumen on* ("We Are on Our Way").

Shooting a scene at the Medem Sanatorium for the film *Mir kumen on* ("We Are on Our Way").

During the late 1930s, Leo-Film, the second largest film company in Poland, produced a sound version of *Tkies-kaf* featuring the Warsaw Yiddish Art Players, the Feniks Company made *The Dybbuk,* and H. Tomaszewski filmed Gordin's *Der yidisher kenig lir* ("The Jewish King Lear"). Between 1937 and 1939, Joseph Green, whose international production company had offices in New York and Warsaw, made four feature films in Poland. He brought a small group of Yiddish actors from America to star in the films, provided subtitles in several languages, and marketed the films internationally. Molly Picon starred in his first production, *Yidl mitn fidl* ("Yidl with His Fiddle"), and Itsik Manger wrote the lyrics for it. Green's production of *A brivele der mamen* ("A Letter to Mother") and Adolph Mann's *On a heym* ("Without a Home") were the last Yiddish films made in Poland before World War II.

Between 1910 and 1940, about one hundred and seventy Yiddish films were made in Poland, Russia, and the United States. About eighty of these were produced in Poland.

Szymon Dzigan and Yisroel Szumacher in the film comedy *On a heym* ("Without a Home"), based on a play by Jacob Gordin. Alter Kacyzne wrote the scenario. The producer was Adolph Mann.

APPENDIX:
Books and Periodicals Consulted

Ain, A. "Świsłocz: Portrait of a Jewish Community in Eastern Europe." *YIVO Annual of Jewish Social Science* **4** (1949): 86–114.

*Alfasi, Y. *Haḥasidut*. Tel Aviv: Sifriat Maariv, 1974.

An-ski, S. "Piśmo v redaktsiiu (o rabotakh etnograficheskoi ekspeditsii)." *Evreiskaia starina* **8** (1915): 239–40.

*Bałaban, M. *Dzielnica żydowska: jej dzieje i zabytki z 40 rycinami w tekście*. Lwów: Towarzystwo Miłośników Przeszłości Lwowa, 1909.

*———. *Zabytki historyczne w Polsce*. Pisma Instytutu Nauk Judaistycznych w Warszawie, vol. 1. Warsaw: Towarzystwo Krzewienia Nauk Judaistycznych w Polsce, 1929.

*———. *Historia Żydów w Krakowie i na Kazimierzu, 1304–1868*. Vol. 1. Cracow: Nadzieja, Towarzystwo ku Wspieraniu Chorej Młodzieży Żydowskiej Szkół Średnich i Wyższych w Krakowie, 1931.

———. *Bibliografia historii Żydów w Polsce i w krajach ościennych za lata 1900–1930*. Vol. 1. Pisma Instytutu Nauk Judaistycznych, vol. 10. Warsaw: Towarzystwo Szerzenia Wiedzy Judaistycznej w Polsce, 1939.

Baron, S. W. *A Social and Religious History of the Jews*. Vol. 16. Poland-Lithuania 1500–1650. 2nd ed. New York: Columbia University Press, 1976.

Baron, S. W., Kahan, A., et al. *Economic History of the Jews*. New York: Schocken Books, 1975.

Bass, D. "Bibliographical List of Memorial Books Published in the Years 1943–1972." *Yad Vashem Studies* **9** (1973): 273–321.

*Baynes, K., ed. *Scoop, Scandal, and Strife: A Study of Photography in Newspapers*. New York: Hastings House, 1971.

*Ben-Ari, R. *Habime*. Chicago: L. M. Stein, 1937.

*Bersohn, M. *Kilka słów o dawniejszych bóżnicach drewnianych w Polsce*. Vol. 2. Cracow: Mathias Bersohn, 1900.

Bornstein, I. *Rzemiosło żydowskie w Polsce*. Warsaw: Instytut Badań Narodowościowych, 1936.

*Borwicz, M. *1000 Years of Jewish Life in Poland*. Paris: Centre d'Etudes Historiques, [1956]. Text in English, French, Hebrew, Polish, Spanish, and Yiddish.

*Boyd, L. A. *Polish Countrysides: Photographs and Narratives*. American Geographical Society Special Publication, no. 20. New York: American Geographical Society, 1937.

Bronsztejn, S. *Ludność żydowska w okresie międzywojennym: Studium statystyczne*. Wrocław: Zakład Narodowy im. Ossolińskich, 1963.

———. "The Jewish Population of Poland in 1931." *Jewish Journal of Sociology* **6** (1964): 3–29.

Carlebach, A. "A German Rabbi Goes East: Emanuel Carlebach's Letters from Warsaw, 1916–1918." *Leo Baeck Institute Year Book* **6** (1961): 60–121.

Chmielewski, S. *Stan szkolnictwa wśród Żydów w Polsce*. Warsaw: Instytut Badań Spraw Narodowościowych, 1937.

Chwila: Dodatek Ilustrowany (Lwów). 1932–1934. Published weekly as a supplement to the Jewish daily *Chwila*.

*Collier, J., Jr. *Visual Anthropology: Photography as a Research Method*. New York: Holt, Rinehart and Winston, 1967.

Czapliński, W. and Ładogórski, T., eds. *Atlas historyczny Polski*. Warsaw: Państwowe Przedsiębiorstwo Wydawnictw Kartograficznych, 1967.

Dawidowicz, L. S., ed. *The Golden Tradition: Jewish Life and*

*Illustrated.

251

Thought in Eastern Europe. New York: Holt, Rinehart and Winston, 1967.

———. The War against the Jews 1933–1945. New York: Holt, Rinehart and Winston, 1975.

Dawidsohn, J. Gminy żydowskie: z tekstami ustaw i rozporządzeń. Warsaw: Klub Posłów Sejmowych Żydowskiej Rady Narodowej, 1931.

Dubnow, S. M. Geshikhte fun khasidizm oyfn yesod fun originele mekoyrim, gedrukte un ksavyadn. 3 vols. Vilna: B. Kleckin for the YIVO Institute for Jewish Research, 1930–1933. Translated from Hebrew by Z. Kalmanowitch.

———. History of the Jews in Russia and Poland from the Earliest Time until the Present Day. Translated from Russian by I. Friedlaender. New York: Ktav, 1975. Reprint of 1916–1920 edition.

*Dziennik Warszawski: Tygodniowy Dodatek Ilustrowany (Warsaw). 1927. Published weekly as a supplement to the Jewish daily Dziennik Warszawski.

Eck, N. "The Educational Institutions of Polish Jewry 1921–1939." Jewish Social Studies 9 (1947): 3–32.

Ehrenpreiz, M., ed. Yidisher folks-kalendar 5656. Lwów: Ekzekutiv-komitet der tsionistisher partey, 1895.

Eisenbach, A. Kwestia równouprawnienia Żydów w Królestwie Polskim. Warsaw: Ksiażka i Wiedza, 1972.

Eisenstein, M. Jewish Schools in Poland 1919–1939. New York: King's Crown Press, 1950.

*Encyclopaedia Judaica. 16 vols. Edited by C. Roth et al. Jerusalem and New York: Macmillan, 1972.

*Evreiskaia entsiklopediia: Svod"

znani" o evreistvie i ego kul'turie v" proshlom" i nastoiashchem". 16 vols. St. Petersburg: Obshchestwo dlia nauchnych evreiskikh izdanii i izdatel'stvo Brokgauz"-Efron, 1908–1913.

Fater, I. Yidishe muzik in poyln tsvishn beyde velt-milkhomes. Tel Aviv: Velt-federatsye fun poylishe yidn, 1970.

*Filmvelt (Warsaw). 1928–1929. Published biweekly.

*Fishberg, M. Die Rassenmerkmale der Juden: Eine Einführung in ihre Anthropologie mit 42 Tafeln in Kunstdruck. Munich: Ernst Reinhardt, 1913.

Fishman, J. A., ed. Studies on Polish Jewry 1919–1939: The Interplay of Social, Economic and Political Factors in the Struggle of a Minority for Its Existence. New York: YIVO Institute for Jewish Research, 1974. Text in English and Yiddish.

*Forward Art Section (New York). 1923–1938. Published weekly as a supplement to The Jewish Daily Forward.

Friedman, F. Dzieje Żydów w Łodzi od początków osadnictwa Żydów do r. 1863: Stosunki ludnościowe, życie gospodarcze, stosunki społeczne. Łódź: Łódzki Oddział Żydowskiego Towarzystwa Krajoznawczego w Polsce, 1935.

Fuks, M. "Początki nowoczesnej prasy żydowskiej w Warszawie (do 1918 r.)." Biuletyn Żydowskiego Instytutu Historycznego 95 (1975): 17–52.

———. "Prasa hebrajska w Warszawie." Biuletyn Żydowskiego Instytutu Historycznego 94 (1975): 3–23.

———. "Prasa żydowska w Warszawie, 1918–1939." Biuletyn Żydowskiego Instytutu Historycznego 85 (1973): 43–78.

Gaster, T. H. Festivals of the Jewish Year: A Modern Interpretation and Guide. New York: Morrow, 1972.

*Gernsheim, H. Creative Photography: Aesthetic Trends 1939–1960. London: Faber and Faber, 1962.

*Gernsheim, H. and A. The History of Photography from the Camera Obscura to the Beginning of the Modern Era. 2nd ed. New York: McGraw-Hill, 1969.

*Gidal, T. N. Modern Photojournalism: Origin and Evolution, 1910–1933. New York: Macmillan, 1973.

Gluck, S. "The Jewish Postcard: Images of Nostalgia," The Metropolitan Post Card Collectors Club Dedicated to Deltiology 30, 6 (1976): 6–7.

*Głos Gminy Żydowskiej (Warsaw), no. 10–11 (1938): 227–337. Special issue: XX-lecie Polski Niepodległej.

*Goldberg, Y. A., ed. Haynt yubiley-bukh 1908–1928. Warsaw: Haynt, 1928.

Golumb, A. A halbe yorhundert yidishe dertsiung. Rio de Janeiro: Monte Scopus, 1957.

Goodman, P. "Rosh Hashanah Greeting Cards," The Rosh Hashanah Anthology. Philadelphia: Jewish Publication Society of America, 1973, pp. 274–279.

*Gorin, B. Di geshikhte fun yidishn teater (tsvey toyzent yor teater bay yidn). 2 vols. 2nd ed., enlarged. New York: Maks N. Meyzel yidisher farlag far literatur un visnshaft, 1923.

*Gothalf, J., ed. Itonut yehudit shehayetah. Tel Aviv: Haigud haolami shel haitonaim hayehudim, 1973.

*Grossman, M. Yidishe vilne in vort un bild: ilustrirter almanakh. Vilna: Hirsh Mets, 1925.

*Haenžiklopediah haivrit: klalit, yehudit, veerežisraelit. 27 volumes to date. Jerusalem: Lehožot enžiklopediot, 1949–.

*Haynt yoyvl-bukh 1908–1938. Warsaw: Haynt, 1938.

Herbst, S. "Wspomnienie o Szymonie Zajczyku." Biuletyn Żydowskiego Instytutu Historycznego 43–44 (1962): 60–62.

Hertz, A. Żydzi w kulturze polskiej. Biblioteka Kultury, no. 66. Paris: Instytut Literacki, 1961.

*Heschel, A. J. The Earth Is the Lord's: The Inner World of the Jews in Eastern Europe. New York: Harper and Row, 1968.

Hilberg, R. The Destruction of European Jews. Chicago: Quadrangle Books, 1961.

Hirszhorn, S. Di geshikhte fun yidn in poyln fun fir-yorikn seym biz der velt-milkhome, 1788–1914. Warsaw: Brider Levin-epshteyn, 1923.

Holzer, J., and Molenda, J. Polska w pierwszej wojnie światowej. Warsaw: Wiedza Powszechna, 1967.

*Hubmann, F. The Jewish Family Album: The Life of a People in Photographs. Boston: Little, Brown, 1975.

*Ilustrirter moment (Warsaw). 1924–1925. Weekly supplement to the daily Der moment.

*Ilustrirte velt: vokhn-zhurnal far literatur, kunst un kultur-fragn (Warsaw). 1919. Published weekly.

*Ilustrirte vokh: zhurnal far vort un bild (Warsaw). 1923–1928. Published weekly.

Janowsky, O. I. The Jews and Minority Rights 1898–1919. Studies in History, Economics and Public Law, no. 384. New York: AMS Press, 1966.

*Jeshurin, E., ed. Vilne: a zaml-bukh gevidmet der shtot vilne. New York: Vilna Branch of the Workmen's Circle, 1935.

*Jewish Encyclopedia: A Descriptive Record of History, Religion, Literature, and Customs of the Jewish People from the Earliest Times to the Present Day. 12 vols. Edited by I. Singer et al. New York and London: Funk and Wagnalls, 1906.

*Jewish Encyclopedic Handbooks and Central Yiddish Culture Organization (CYCO). The Jewish People: Past and Present. 4 vols. New York: Marstin Press, 1946–1955.

Johnpoll, B. K. The Politics of Futility: The General Jewish Workers of Poland 1917–1943. Ithaca: Cornell University Press, 1967.

*Jüdisches Lexikon: Ein enzyklopädisches Handbuch des jüdischen Wissens in vier Bänden. 4 vols. Edited by G. Herlitz and B. Kirschner. Berlin: Jüdischer Verlag, 1927–1930.

*Jussim, E. Visual Communication and the Graphic Arts: Photographic Technologies in the Nineteenth Century. New York: R. R. Bowker, 1974.

Kazdan, C. S. Di geshikhte fun yidishn shulvezn in umophengikn poyln. Mexico City: Gezelshaft "kultur un hilf," 1947.

———. Fun kheyder un "shkoles" biz tsisho: dos ruslendishe yidntum in gerangl far shul, shprakh, kultur. Mexico City: Imprenta Moderna, 1956.

———., ed. Medemsanatorye-bukh. Tel Aviv: Hamenorah, 1971.

Khayes, S. "Nemen fun galitsishe erter in yidishe mekoyrim un inem folks-loshn." YIVO bleter 7 (1934): 229–42, 286.

*Kin-te-rad: ilustrirter vokhnblat far kino, teater, un radyo (Warsaw). 1926–1927. Published weekly.

Komitet far der oysgabe "Yidn in poyln." Di yidn in poyln fun di eltste tsaytn biz der tsveyter velt-milkhome. New York: Undzer tsayt, 1946.

*Komitet Uczczenia Pierwszego Prezydenta Rzeczypospolitej Polskiej Ś. P. Gabrjela Narutowicza. Gabrjel Narutowicz, pierwszy prezydent Rzeczypospolitej: Księga pamiątkowa. Warsaw: Komitet Uczczenia Pierwszego Prezydenta Rzeczypospolitej Polskiej Ś. P. Gabrjela Narutowicza, 1925.

*Krajoznawstwo-Wiadomości Ż. T. K.: Czasopismo Żydowskiego Towarzystwa Krajoznawczego Poświęcone Zagadnieniom Turystyki, Krajoznawstwa oraz Badaniom Osiedli Żydowskich w Polsce (Warsaw). 1935–1937. Published monthly. Text in Polish and Yiddish.

*Kułakowski, T. Gdyby Hitler zwyciężył. . . . Warsaw: Książka i Wiedza, 1960.

Landau, Z. and Tomaszewski, J. "Społeczeństwo Drugiej Rzeczypospolitej (Uwagi polemiczne)." Przegląd Historyczny 2 (1970): 317–22.

———. Robotnicy przemysłowi w Polsce: Materialne warunki bytu w latach 1918–1939. Warsaw: Książka i Wiedza, 1971.

Langnas, S. Żydzi a studia akademickie w Polsce w latach 1921–1931 (Studium statystyczne). Lwów: Centrala Żydowskich Akademickich Towarzystw Samopomocowych Środowiska Lwowskiego, 1933.

Leksikon fun der nayer yidisher literatur. 7 volumes to date. New York: Congress for Jewish Culture, 1956–.

Lestchinsky, J. "Aspects of the

Sociology of Polish Jewry." *Jewish Social Studies* **28** (1966): 195–211.

———. "The Industrial and Social Structure of the Jewish Population of Interbellum Poland." *YIVO Annual of Jewish Social Science* **11** (1956–1957): 243–69.

———. "The Jews in the Cities of the Republic of Poland." *YIVO Annual of Jewish Social Science* **1** (1946): 156–77.

Lestchinsky, J., ed. *Shriftn far ekonomik un statistik*, vol. 1. Berlin: YIVO Institute for Jewish Research, 1928.

Levitats, I. *The Jewish Community in Russia 1772–1844.* New York: Octagon Books, 1970. Reprint of 1943 edition.

*Leyda, J. *Kino: A History of Russian and Soviet Film.* New York: Macmillan, 1960.

Liptzin, S. *A History of Yiddish Literature.* Middle Village, New York: Jonathan David Publishers, 1972.

Literarishe bleter: ilustrirte vokhnshrift far literatur, teater un kunst (Warsaw). 1924–1939. Published weekly.

*Loukomski, G. *Jewish Art in European Synagogues (from the Middle Ages to the 18th Century).* London: Hutchinson, 1947.

*Łoza, S., ed. *Czy wiesz kto to jest?* Warsaw: Główna Księgarnia Wojskowa, 1938.

Madison, C. A. *Yiddish Literature—Its Scope and Major Writers.* New York: Schocken Books, 1968.

Mahler, R. "Antisemitism in Poland". In *Essays on Antisemitism*, edited by K. S. Pinson. Jewish Social Studies Publication, no. 2, pp. 111–42. New York: Conference of Jewish Relations, 1946.

———. "The Economic Background of Jewish Emigra-tion from Galicia to the United States." *YIVO Annual of Jewish Social Science* **7** (1952): 255–67.

———. "Jews in Public Service and the Liberal Professions in Poland 1918–1939." *Jewish Social Studies* **6** (1944): 291–350.

———. "Shemoth yehudiim shel mekomoth bepolin hayishanah." *Reshumoth*, n.s. **5** (1953): 146–61.

Manger, I., Turkow, J., and Perenson, M., eds. *Yidisher teater in eyrope tsvishn beyde velt-milkhomes (materyaln tsu der geshikhte fun yidishn teater): poyln.* New York: Congress for Jewish Culture, 1968.

Matis, D. "Tsu der geshikhte fun yidishe films." *YKUF—almanakh 1961*, edited by N. Meisel, pp. 439–65. New York: Yidisher kultur farband (YKUF), 1961.

Maursberg, S. *Szkolnictwo powszechne dla mniejszości narodowych w Polsce w latach 1918–1939.* Wrocław: Zakład Narodowy im. Ossolińskich, 1968.

Mendelsohn, E. *Class Struggle in the Pale: The Formative Years of the Jewish Workers' Movement in Tsarist Russia.* Cambridge: Cambridge University Press, 1970.

———."The Dilemma of Jewish Politics in Poland: Four Responses." In *Jews and Non-Jews in Eastern Europe 1918–1945*, edited by B. Vago and G. L. Mosse, pp. 203–19. New York and Toronto: Halstead Press, 1974.

———. "The Politics of Agudas-Yisroel in Inter-War Poland." *Soviet Jewish Affairs* **2** (1972): 47–60.

*Miron, D. *A Traveler Disguised: The Rise of Modern Yiddish Fiction in the Nineteenth Century.* New York: Schocken Books, 1973.

Nasz Przegląd Ilustrowany (Warsaw). 1925–1930. Published weekly as a supplement to the Jewish daily *Nasz Przegląd*.

Naye ilustrirte vokh: zhurnal far vort un bild (Warsaw). 1925. Published weekly.

*Newhall, B. *The History of Photography from 1839 to the Present Day.* 4th ed, revised and enlarged. New York: Museum of Modern Art and George Eastman House, 1964.

*Piechotka, M. and K. *Wooden Synagogues.* Warsaw: Arkady, 1959.

Pollner, M. *Emigracja i przewartościowanie Żydów polskich.* Warsaw: Majer Pollner, 1939.

Polonsky, A. *Politics in Independent Poland 1921–1939: The Crisis of Constitutional Government.* Oxford: Oxford University Press, 1972.

Polski słownik biograficzny. 20 volumes to date. Cracow and Wrocław: Polska Akademja Umiejętności–Polska Akademia Nauk, 1935–.

Rabinowitsch, W. Z. *Lithuanian Hasidism.* Translated from Hebrew by M. B. Dagut. New York: Schocken Books, 1971.

*Ran, L. *Jerusalem of Lithuania: Illustrated and Documented.* 3 vols. New York: Vilno Album Committee, 1974. Text in English, Hebrew, Russian, and Yiddish.

Raviv, M. See Vorobeichic, M.

*Rechtman, A. *Yidishe etnografye un folklor: zikhroynes vegn der etnografisher ekspeditsye, ongefirt fun Sh. An-ski.* Buenos Aires: YIVO Institute for Jewish Research, 1958.

Reddaway, W. F., ed. *The Cambridge History of Poland.* 2 vols. New York: Octagon Books, 1971. Reprint of 1941 (vol. 1) and 1950 (vol. 2) editions.

*Reisen, Z. *Leksikon fun der yidisher literatur, prese un filologye.*

4 vols. 2nd ed., revised. Vilna: B. Kleckin, 1927–1929.

*Roman-tsaytung: a ilustrirtes vokhnblat far literatur, kunst un visnshaft (Warsaw). 1907–1908. Published weekly.

Romer, E., ed. Geograficzno-statystyczny Atlas Polski. Lwów and Warsaw: Książnica Polska Towarzystwa Nauczycieli Szkół Wyższych, 1921.

*Ruppin, A. Soziologie der Juden. 2 vols. Berlin: Jüdischer Verlag, 1930.

*Sandel, J. Plastishe kunst bay yidn in poyln. Warsaw: Yidish bukh, 1964.

*———. Umgekumene yidishe kinstler in poyln. 2 vols. Warsaw: Yidish bukh, 1957.

*Sandrow, N. Vagabond Stars: A World History of Yiddish Theater. New York: Harper and Row, 1977.

Schauss, H. Guide to Jewish Holidays: History and Observance. Translated from Yiddish by S. Jaffe. New York: Schocken Books, 1970.

Schiper, I. Dzieje handlu żydowskiego na ziemiach polskich. Warsaw: Centrala Związku Kupców, 1937.

Schiper, I., Tartakower, A., and Hafftka, A., eds. Żydzi w Polsce Odrodzonej: Działalność społeczna, gospodarcza, oświatowa i kulturalna. 2 vols. Warsaw: Żydzi w Polsce Odrodzonej, [1932–1933].

Scholem, G. G. Major Trends in Jewish Mysticism. New York: Schocken Books, 1961.

Schorr, M. Organizacja Żydów w Polsce (od najdawniejszych czasów aż do r. 1772). Lwów: M. Schorr, 1899.

Segal, S. The New Poland and the Jews. New York: Lee Furman, 1938.

*Seidman, H. Szlakiem nauki talmudycznej: Wiedza judaistyczna a Wyższa Uczelnia w Lublinie. Warsaw: F. Hoesick, 1937.

Shatzky, J. "Institutional Aspects of Jewish Life in the Second Half of the 19th Century." YIVO Annual of Jewish Social Science 10 (1955): 9–44.

———. "Warsaw Jews in the Polish Cultural Life of the Early 19th Century." YIVO Annual of Jewish Social Science 5 (1950): 41–54.

———. Yidishe bildungs-politik in poyln fun 1806 biz 1866. New York: YIVO Institute for Jewish Research, 1943.

Shtern, Y. Kheyder un besmedresh. New York: YIVO Institute for Jewish Research, 1950.

*Der shtral (Warsaw). 1910–1911. Published weekly.

*Shulman, A. The Old Country. New York: Charles Scribner's Sons, 1974.

*Siuchniński, M., ed. Miasta polskie w tysiącleciu. 2 vols. Wrocław: Zakład Narodowy im. Ossolińskich, 1965, 1967.

*Staff, F. The Picture Postcard and Its Origins. New York: Praeger, 1966.

Stankiewicz, E. "Yiddish Place Names in Poland." in The Field of Yiddish: Studies in Language, Folklore, and Literature. Second collection. Edited by U. Weinreich, pp. 158–81. The Hague: Mouton, 1965.

Szajn, I. "Bibliografia dzienników i czasopism żydowskich wydawanych w Polsce w latach 1918–1939 w języku polskim." Biuletyn Żydowskiego Instytutu Historycznego 78 (1971): 107–32.

———. "Bibliografia wydawnictw nieperiodycznych dotyczących instytucji i organizacji społecznych działających w Polsce w latach 1918–1939 (wydawanych w języku polskim)." Biuletyn Żydowskiego Instytutu Historycznego 95 (1975): 106–12.

———. "Bibliografia żydowskiej prasy młodzieżowej wydawanej w Polsce w latach 1918–1939, w języku polskim." Biuletyn Żydowskiego Instytutu Historycznego 94 (1975): 103–13.

———. Bibliografye fun oysgabes aroysgegebn durkh di arbeter-parteyen in poyln in di yorn 1918–1939. Warsaw: Yidish bukh, 1963.

*Szarkowski, J. The Photographer's Eye. New York: Museum of Modern Art, 1966.

Szturm de Szterm, E. Statistical Atlas of Poland. Edinburgh and London: Polish Ministry of Information, n.d.

*Szulc, M. Materiały do historii fotografii polskiej. Vol. 1. Bibliografia 1836–1956. Wrocław: Zakład Narodowy im. Ossolińskich, 1956.

Tartakower, A. Emigracja Żydów z Polski. Warsaw: Instytut Badań Spraw Narodowościowych, 1939.

*Teater-velt: ilustrirtes vokhnblat far teater, literatur, kunst, visnshaft un farvaylung (Warsaw). 1908–1909. Published weekly.

Tobias, H. J. The Jewish Bund in Russia from Its Origins to 1905. Stanford: Stanford University Press, 1972.

Turkow-Grudberg, I. Varshe. dos vigele fun yidishn teater. Warsaw: Yidish bukh, 1956.

———. Yidish teater in poyln. Warsaw: Yidish bukh, 1951.

*The Universal Jewish Encyclopedia: An Authoritative and Popular Presentation of Jews and Judaism Since the Earliest Times. 10 vols. Edited by I. Landman. New York: The

Universal Jewish Encyclopedia, 1939–1943.

*Urbach, J. K. *Udział Żydów w walce o niepodległość Polski*. Łódź: Związek Uczestników Walk o Niepodległość Polski, 1938.

Veltshpigl: vokhnblat far ale (Warsaw). 1927–1939. Published weekly.

Veltshpigl (Warsaw). 1924. Published irregularly.

*Verlag des Deutschen Offizierblattes. *Das Generalgouvernement Warschau: Eine Bilderreihe aus der Zeit des Weltkrieges herausgegeben von Kaizerlich Deutschen Generalgouvernement Warschau. Mit 315 Bildern*. Oldenburg: Druck und Verlag von Gerhard Stalling, 1918.

Vishniac, M. "Antisemitism in Tsarist Russia: A Study in Government-Fostered Antisemitism." In *Essays on Antisemitism*, edited by K. S. Pinson. Jewish Social Studies Publication, no. 2, pp. 79–110. New York: Conference of Jewish Relations, 1946.

*Vishniac, R. *Polish Jews: A Pictorial Record*. New York: Schocken Books, 1949.

*——. *Roman Vishniac*. International Center for Photography Library of Photographers, vol. 6. New York: Grossman Publishers, 1974.

*Vorobeichic, M. [Raviv, M.] *The Ghetto Lane in Vilna: 65 Pictures*. Zurich: Orell Fussli Publishers, 1931. Text in English and Hebrew.

Wandycz, P. S. *The Lands of Partitioned Poland. 1795–1918*. A History of Central Europe, vol. 7. Seattle: University of Washington Press, 1974.

Wasiutynski, B. *Ludność żydowska w Polsce w wiekach XIX i XX: Studium statystyczne*. Warsaw: Kasa im. Mianowskiego, Instytut Popierania Nauki, 1930.

Weinreich, M. *Geshikhte fun der yidisher shprakh: bagrifn, faktn, metodn*. 4 vols. New York: YIVO Institute for Jewish Research, 1973.

Weinreich U. and B. *Yiddish Language and Folklore: A Selective Bibliography for Research*. Janua Linguarum, no. 10. The Hague: Mouton, 1959.

Weinryb, B. D. "East European Jewry (Since the Partitions, 1772–1795)." In *The Jews: Their History*, 4th ed., edited by Louis Finkelstein, pp. 343–98. New York: Schocken Books, 1970.

——. *The Jews of Poland: A Social and Economic History of the Jewish Community in Poland from 1100 to 1800*. Philadelphia: Jewish Publication Society of America, 1973.

*Weissenberg, S. *Die südrussische Juden: Eine anthropometrische Studie mit Berücksichtigung der allgemeinen Entwicklungsgesetze*. Braunschweig: Friedrich Vieweg und Sohn, 1895.

Wiadomości Z. T. K.: Organ Zarządu Głównego Żydowskiego Towarzystwa Krajoznawczego w Polsce (Warsaw). 1930–1933. Published monthly (irregular). Text in Polish and Yiddish.

Wielka encyklopedia powszechna. 13 vols. Warsaw: Państwowe Wydawnictwo Naukowe, 1962–1970.

Wielka ilustrowana encyklopedia powszechna. 22 vols. Cracow: Gutenberg, 1929–1938.

Wiener, M. *Tsu der geshikhte fun der yidisher literatur in 19-tn yorhundert (etyudn un materyaln)*. 2 vols. New York: Yidisher kultur farband (YKUF), 1945–1946.

Wischnitzer, M. *A History of Jewish Crafts and Guilds*. Middle Village, New York: Jonathan David Publishers, 1965.

*Wischnitzer, R. *The Architecture of the European Synagogue*. Philadelphia: Jewish Publication Society of America, 1964.

*Wulman, L., ed. *In Fight for the Health of the Jewish People (50 Years of OSE)*. New York: World Union OSE and American Committee of OSE, 1968. Text in English, French, Hebrew, and Yiddish.

Wynot, E. D. "A 'Necessary Cruelty': The Emergence of Official Anti-Semitism in Poland, 1936–1939." *American Historical Review* **76** (1971): 1035–1058.

*Yarmolinsky, A. "Tsu der ikonografye fun mizrakh-eyropeyishe yidn (16 bilder)." *YIVO-bleter* **28** (1946): 254–72.

Yidishe bilder (Riga). 1937–1939. Published weekly.

Yidishe bine: ilustrirter zhurnal baym yidishn artistn-fareyn in poyln (Warsaw). 1924. Published irregularly.

Żarnowski, J. *Społeczeństwo Drugiej Rzeczypospolitej*. Warsaw: Książka i Wiedza, 1973.

*Ždżarski, W. *Historia fotografii warszawskiej*. Warsaw: Państwowe Wydawnictwo Naukowe, 1974.

*Zineman, J. ed. *Almanach gmin żydowskich w Polsce*, vol. 1. Warsaw: Nasze Życie, 1939.

——. *Almanach szkolnictwa żydowskiego w Polsce*, Vol. 1. Warsaw: Renesans, 1938.

Zwischen Styr und Bug. Berlin: Meisenbach Riffarth, n.d.

*Zylbercwaig, Z., comp. and ed. *Leksikon fun yidishn teater*. 6 vols. New York and Mexico City: Alisheva for the Hebrew Actors Union of America, 1931–1969.

Statistical and Toponymic Materials

TABLE 1.
Toponymy and Population of Settlements Where Photographs in This Volume Were Taken***

SETTLEMENT		PROVINCE	TOTAL POPULATION	JEWISH POPULATION	
YIDDISH NAME	POLISH NAME			NUMBER	PERCENT
Baranovitsh	Baranowicze	Nowogródek	11,471	6,605	57.6
Benshin	Zbąszyn	Poznań	5,432	54	1.4
Bidgosh or Bidgoshtsh	Bydgoszcz	Poznań	87,848	745	0.8
Bobev	Bobowa	Cracow	1,422	565	39.7
Bogorye	Bogorja	Kielce	1,185	450	38.0
Braynsk	Brańsk	Białystok	3,739	2,165	57.9
Brezhin or Bzhezhin	Brzeziny	Łódź	10,633	4,979	46.8
Brisk (D'Lite)	Brześć nad Bugiem	Polesie	29,553	15,630	52.9
Brod	Brody	Tarnopol	10,867	7,222	66.3
Byale	Biała	Cracow	7,746	1,363	17.6
Byalistok	Białystok	Białystok	76,792	39,602	51.6
Dantsk, di fraye shtot	Gdańsk-Danzig	The Free City of Gdańsk-Danzig	235,000	5,873	2.5
Dlugeshedle	Długosiodło	Lwów	1,744	801	45.9
Dobzhin or Dobrin oyf der Vaysl	Dobrzyń nad Wisłą	Warsaw	2,693	775	28.8
Ger	Góra Kalwaria	Warsaw	5,496	2,961	53.9
Gombin	Gąbin	Warsaw	5,777	2,564	44.4
Grayeve	Grajewo	Białystok	7,346	2,834	34.4
Grodne	Grodno	Białystok	34,694	18,697	53.9
Groys Vileyke or Vileyke	Wilejka	Vilna	3,417	710	20.8
Khelem	Chełm	Lublin	23,219	12,064	52.0
Khoderev	Chodorów	Lwów	4,206	1,230	29.2
Klesov	Klesów	Wołyń			
Kleyn-Minsk or Minsk	Mińsk Mazowiecki	Warsaw	10,518	4,130	39.3
Kosev or Koseve	Kosów	Stanisławów	4,234	2,166	51.2
Kremenits	Krzemieniec	Wołyń	16,068	6,616	41.2

***Unless otherwise indicated the population figures are based on the census of 1921. In those cases where the census of 1921 did not contain information, the local census of 1919 (*) and general census of 1931 (**) were used.

TABLE 1. — Continued

SETTLEMENT		PROVINCE	TOTAL POPULATION	JEWISH POPULATION	
YIDDISH NAME	POLISH NAME			NUMBER	PERCENT
Krenits	Krynica-Zdrój	Cracow	2,341	1,023	43.7
Kroke or Kruke	Cracow	Cracow	183,706	45,299	24.6
Kuzmir	Kazimierz nad Wisłą	Lublin	3,407	1,382	40.6
Lakhve	Łachwa	Polesie	3,420	1,126	32.9
Laskarev	Łaskarzew	Lublin	3,411	1,352	39.6
Lemberg or Lemberik	Lwów	Lwów	219,388	76,854	35.0
Lodzh	Łódź	Łódź	451,974	156,155	34.5
Lomze or Lomzhe	Łomża	Białystok	22,014	9,131	41.5
Losk	Łask	Łódź	4,890	2,623	53.6
Loytsk	Łuck	Wołyń	21,157	14,860	70.2
Lublin	Lublin	Lublin	94,412	37,337	39.5
Lyubtsh	Lubcza	Nowogródek	559*	327*	58.5
Matshevits	Maciejowice	Lublin	1,992	799	40.1
Medzeshin	Miedzeszyn	Warsaw			
Mlave	Mława	Warsaw	17,003	5,923	34.8
Modzhits or Demblin	Dęblin	Lublin			
Nasheltsk	Nasielsk	Warsaw	5,030	2,691	53.5
Nay-shtetl	Nowe Miasto	Warsaw	3,761	1,667	44.3
Nay Vileyke	Nowa Wilejka	Vilna			
Nyementshin	Niemenczyn	Vilna			
Orle	Orla	Białystok	1,518	1,167	76.9
Ostre	Ostróg	Wołyń	12,975	7,991	61.6
Otvotsk	Otwock	Warsaw	8,560	5,408	63.2
Patshenev	Pacanów	Kielce	2,598	1,689	65.0
Pinsk	Pińsk	Polesie	23,468	17,513	74.6
Plinsk	Płońsk	Warsaw	9,220	4,460	48.4
Pshiskhe	Przysucha	Kielce	3,238	2,153	66.5
Pshitik	Przytyk	Kielce	2,302	1,852	80.5
Pushtsha Kampinoska	Puszcza Kampinoska	Warsaw			
Rakhev	Annopol	Lublin	1,714	1,251	73.0
Retin or Rotin	Rohatyn	Stanisławów	5,736	2,233	38.9
Rosokhetsh	Rosochacz	Lwów			
Rovne	Równe	Wołyń	30,482	21,702	71.2
Rubeshoyv	Hrubieszów	Lublin	9,598	5,679	59.2
Shershev	Szereszów	Polesie	3,310	1,341	40.5
Shydlovtse	Szydłowiec	Kielce			
Sislevitsh	Świsłocz	Białystok	2,935	1,959	66.7
Skernevits	Skierniewice	Warsaw	15,265	4,333	28.4
Smargon	Smorgonie	Vilna			
Stanislov	Stanisławów	Stanisławów	28,204	15,860	56.2
Stashev	Staszów	Kielce	8,357	4,704	57.5

TABLE 1. — Continued

SETTLEMENT		PROVINCE	TOTAL POPULATION	JEWISH POPULATION	
YIDDISH NAME	POLISH NAME			NUMBER	PERCENT
Striy	Stryj	Stanisławów	27,358	10,988	40.2
Tarnepol	Tarnopol	Tarnopol	30,891	13,768	44.6
Torne or Tarne	Tarnów	Cracow	35,347	15,608	44.2
Tshenstekhev or Tshenstokhov	Częstochowa	Kielce	80,473	22,663	28.2
Tshortkev	Czortków	Tarnopol	5,191	3,314	63.8
Varshe	Warszawa	Warsaw			
Vilne	Wilno	Vilna	195,071**	55,506**	
Visoke	Wysokie Litewskie	Polesie	2,100	1,902	90.6
Visotsk	Wysock	Wołyń	2,978	893	30.0
Vlotsheve	Włoszczowa	Kielce	5,479	2,910	53.1
Vlotslavek or Alt Lesle	Włocławek	Warsaw	40,281	9,595	23.8
Volemin	Wołomin	Warsaw	6,248	3,079	49.3
Volkovisk	Wołkowysk	Białystok	11,100	5,130	46.2
Volozhn	Wołożyn	Nowogródek	2,630	1,434	54.5
Volpe	Wołpa	Białystok	1,687*	983*	
Vonvelnits	Wąwolnica	Lublin	3,003	1,043	34.7
Yablone	Jabłonna-Legjonowo	Warsaw	2,081	572	21.7
Yezhor	Jeziory	Białystok	1,730*	1,162*	
Yidishe yezhorane	Jeziorany Żydowskie	Wołyń	2,861	1,817	63.5
Zabludeve or Zabludove	Zabłudów	Białystok			
Zalishtshik	Zaleszczyki	Białystok	4,014	2,485	61.9
Zamishtsh	Zamość	Lublin	24,241**	10,265**	
Zhabne	Żabno	Cracow	1,228	361	29.4
Zhekhlin	Żychlin	Warsaw	7,098	2,701	39.5

TABLE 2.
Ethnic Composition of the Population in Poland in 1931*

NATIONALITY	ABSOLUTE NUMBER	PERCENTAGE OF TOTAL POPULATION
Poles	20,644,000	64
Ukrainians	5,114,000	16
Jews	3,114,000	10
Byelorussians	1,954,000	6
Germans	780,000	3
Others (Russians, Lithuanians, Slovaks, Armenians, Gypsies, Tatars, etc.)	310,000	1
Total population	31,916,000	100%

*This table is based on Tables 36 and 37 in Landau and Tomaszewski 1970 and on Table 1 in Landau and Tomaszewski 1970.

TABLE 3.
Occupational Distribution of Jews and Non-Jews
in Poland, 1921 and 1931*

OCCUPATION	PERCENTAGE OF TOTAL POPULATION		PERCENTAGE OF JEWS	
	1921	1931	1921	1931
Agriculture	63.8	60.9	5.7	4.4
Manufacturing	17.2	19.2	39.5	42.2
Trade	6.2	5.9	41.2	36.6
Transportation and communication	3.4	3.6	3.5	4.5
Free professions and government	3.7	4.1	4.1	5.1
Service (mainly domestic)	1.1	1.4	2.3	1.8
Other	4.6	4.9	3.7	5.4
Total	100%	100%	100%	100%

*This table is based on Żarnowski 1973: 22 and Bronsztejn 1963: 20.

TABLE 4.
Total and Jewish Population of Poland and Percentage of Jews in Poland
Declaring Yiddish or Hebrew as Mother Tongue*

REGIONS, PROVINCES, AND MAJOR CITIES	TOTAL POPULATION		JEWISH POPULATION		
	NUMBER OF INHABITANTS	PERCENTAGE OF TOTAL POPULATION IN POLAND	NUMBER OF JEWS	PERCENTAGE OF JEWISH POPULATION IN POLAND	PERCENTAGE OF JEWS IN EACH LOCATION WHO DECLARED YIDDISH OR HEBREW AS MOTHER TONGUE
Central Provinces (formerly Congress Poland)	11,733,769	36.7	1,581,638	50.5	93.0
WARSAW	3,701,126	11.6	571,783	18.3	95.8
City of Warsaw	(1,171,898)	(3.6)	(352,659)	(11.3)	(94.4)
ŁÓDŹ	2,632,010	8.2	378,495	11.9	94.9
City of Łódź	(604,629)	(1.8)	(202,497)	(6.3)	(94.6)
KIELCE	2,935,697	9.2	317,020	10.2	96.2
LUBLIN	2,464,936	7.7	314,340	10.1	82.5
Northeastern Provinces (Region of Lite)	5,108,869	16.0	505,021	16.2	97.8
VILNA	1,275,939	4.0	110,796	3.6	98.2
City of Vilna	(195,071)	(0.6)	(55.006)	(1.8)	(99.2)
NOWOGRÓDEK	1,057,147	3.3	82,872	2.7	92.9
BIAŁYSTOK	1,643,844	5.1	197,365	6.3	98.8
POLESIE	1,131,939	3.5	113,988	3.6	99.1

*Figures are based on the census of 1931.

TABLE 4. — Continued

REGIONS, PROVINCES, AND MAJOR CITIES	TOTAL POPULATION		JEWISH POPULATION		
	NUMBER OF INHABITANTS	PERCENTAGE OF TOTAL POPULATION IN POLAND	NUMBER OF JEWS	PERCENTAGE OF JEWISH POPULATION IN POLAND	PERCENTAGE OF JEWS IN EACH LOCATION WHO DECLARED YIDDISH OR HEBREW AS MOTHER TONGUE
Southern Provinces (Regions of Volhynia and Galicia)	10,591,476	33.18	997,678	32.1	75.7
WOŁYŃ	2,085,574	6.53	207,792	6.7	98.9
LWÓW	3,127,409	9.80	342,405	11.0	68.0
City of Lwów	(312,231)	(0.98)	(99,595)	(3.2)	(75.6)
TARNOPOL	1,600,406	5.01	134,117	4.3	58.8
STANISŁAWÓW	1,480,285	4.64	139,746	4.5	78.8
CRACOW	2,297,802	7.20	173,618	5.6	73.7
City of Cracow	(219,286)	(0.69)	(56,515)	(1.8)	(81.0)
Western Provinces (Regions of Great Poland, Pomerania, and Silesia)	4,481,665	14.03	29,596	1.0	39.1
POMERANIA	1,080,138	3.38	3,447	0.1	54.7
POZNAŃ	2,106,500	6.60	7,211	0.3	44.6
City of Poznań	(246,470)	(0.72)	(1,954)	(0.1)	(54.6)
SILESIA	1,295,027	4.05	18,938	0.6	34.1
Totals	31,915,779	(99.91)	3,113,933	99.8	

TABLE 5.
Enrollment of Jews in Educational Institutions in Poland, 1934–1935*

TYPE OF SCHOOL AND AFFILIATION	NUMBER OF SCHOOLS	ENROLLMENTS
Non-Jewish		
STATE, MUNICIPAL, and PRIVATE		
elementary		425,566
secondary		29,822
vocational		6,994
special (for the disabled)		1,607
university		7,114
Total		471,103

*This table is based on Zineman 1938, Chmielewski 1937, Kazdan 1947, and Mauersberg 1968. The number of enrollments is greater than the number of students because one person might enroll at more than one institution; for example, one student might attend a public elementary school in the morning and a Jewish school in the afternoon. According to the census of 1931, the total number of Jews between the ages of three and nineteen in Poland was 1,056,556.

TABLE 5. — Continued

TYPE OF SCHOOL AND AFFILIATION	NUMBER OF SCHOOLS	ENROLLMENTS
Jewish		
TARBUT (Zionist)		
kindergarten and elementary	255	35,764
secondary and vocational	10	2,557
evening	4	6,229
Total	269	44,550
CYSHO (Bund, Labor Zionist, Folkist, and others)		
kindergarten and elementary	97	10,256
secondary	2	650
evening	70	4,580
Total	169	15,486
SHUL-KULT (Labor Zionist and others)		
kindergarten and elementary	13	2,026
evening	3	317
Total	16	2,343
JEWISH SECONDARY SCHOOL FEDERATION (officially nonpartisan but Zionist-influenced)		8,300
YAVNEH (Mizrachi)		
kindergarten and elementary	220	
secondary	3	
yeshivah	4	
rabbinical seminary	2	
Total	229	15,923
HOREV (*Agudas yisroel*)		
kheyder and Talmud Torah	557	61,328
yeshivah	197	18,758
Total	754	80,086
BETH JACOB (*Agudas yisroel*)		20,000
PRIVATE		
kheyder		40,000
secondary (gymnasium and lyceum)	147	8,232**
Total		48,232
VOCATIONAL		
ORT		4,427***
ICA		2,942***
WUZET		1,933***
Total		9,302
Total number of enrollments in Jewish schools		244,452
Total number of Jewish enrollments		725,655

**1937–1938
***1935–1936

TABLE 6.

The Jewish Press in Poland, 1938–1939

Provinces and number of cities in each	Number of newspapers and periodicals	Languages: Yiddish	Hebrew	Polish	German	Bilingual	Frequency: Dailies — Number	Dailies — Circulation	Weeklies	Other periodicals	Issued irr.	Type: General	Socio-political	Cultural	Scientific	Trade unions and professions	Youth	Sport	Affiliation: Zionists	Bund	Agudas Yisroel	Folkists	Communists	Communal, educational, and other organizations
Warsaw, city of	103	83	3	14		3	11	400,000	21	46	25	45	7	8	5	23	11	4	18	7	3	1	2	72
Warsaw / 1	1					1					1	1												1
Łódź / 5	16	15		1			2	17,000	6	5	3	6	4	2		3		1	1		1			14
Kielce / 6	13	12		1			1	3,000	8	1	3	12	1						1	1	1			10
Lublin / 6	9	9					1	1,500	6		2	8	1						1	1		1		6
Vilna / 1	18	18					6	42,000	2	5	5	7			6	2	3		2			1		15
Nowogródek / 3	10	10							9		1	10							1			1		8
Białystok / 4	14	14					7	16,400	2	2	3	11	2	1					1	1				12
Polesie / 3	6	6					1	2,000	4		1	3	2	1					1					5
Wołyń / 6	9	9					1	3,000	7	1		6	1	2								1		8
Lwów / 2	15	7		7		1	2	10,000	7	4	2	10	3			1	1		4					11
Tarnopol / 1	1	1									1	1							1					
Stanisławów / 2	11	8		3					5	2	4	7	2	1			1		2			1		8
Cracow / 2	6	3		3			1	18,000	5			3	1			1	1		2					4
Pomerania / 3	9	6		2	1				7	1	1	8	1						1	1		1		6
Poznań / 1	2	2							2			2							1	1				1
Silesia / 1	3	1			1	1			2	1		3							1	1				2
Total / 48	246	204	3	31	2	6	33	512,900	93	68	52	143	25	15	11	30	17	5	37	10	5	7	2	185

INDEX

Index of Names*

Abramovitch, Raphael, 25, 32, 33, 36, 46, 48, 52, 57, 59, 69, 73, 77, 78, 79, 81, 82, 90, 92, 93, 100, 142, 158, 159, 162, 167, 203, 217

Abramovitsh, Shalom Jacob. *See* Mendele Moykher Sforim

Abramowicz, Dina, vi

Achtentuch, Herbert, 59

Adam haKohen. *See* Lebensohn, J. L.

Ain, Avrom, 11, 114

Ajdelman, Yudl, 11

Albert, Joseph, 3

Aleksandrowitz, Wilhelm, 29, 71

Alpert, Zalman, vi

Alter, Abraham Mordecai, 72

American Photographer, 177

An-ski, S., 17, 220, 237

Apfelbaum, M., 27

Apollo, 121

Archer, Frederick Scott, 3

Asch, Sholem, 222, 241

Ba'al Shem Tov, 74

Bałaban, Majer, 16, 61, 67, 215, 217

Bar Kokhba, 88

Barwiński, Henryk, 122

Begell, Wilhelm, 245

Bella Bellarina. *See* Rubinlicht, Bella

Beloy, G., 218

Ben-Gurion, David, 190

Berlin, M., 17

Bersohn, Mathias, 16, 163

Beyer, Karol, 3, 5, 11

Bialik, Chaim Nachman, 237, 242

Bobover rebe. See Halberstam, Ben-Zion

Bojm, Henryk, 29, 143, 182, 247

Borkowski, W., 14, 55

Borwicz, Michał, 35

Bracia Bietkowsky, 205

Brandsteter, 161

Breitbart, Zishe, 23

Broderson, Moshe, 225, 240, 245

Broudner, 122, 220, 235

Buloff, Joseph, 241

Buzgan, Khevel, 237, 247

Bychowski, Zygmunt, 189

Chagall, Marc, 184

Charney, Daniel, 184

Charney, Samuel. *See* Niger, Samuel

Chmielnicki, Bogdan, 70

Clemenceau, Georges, 22

Condell, Luba, vii

Copernicus, Nicholas, 50

Curie, Marie, 21

Curie, Pierre, 21

Cyn, Berl, 100

Czernichow, M., 215

Daguerre, Louis Jacques Mandé, 3

Dancygerkron, M., 31

David ben Shalom, 57

Dawidowicz, Szymon, vi

Demuth, Leopold, 23

Diamand, Herman, 187

Dick, Isaac Meir, 218

Dineson, Jacob, 218, 219, 220

Disderi, Andre, 5

Dobkin, Toby Blum, vii

Dobroszycki, Felicja, viii

Dobroszycki, Joanna, viii

Dobroszycki, Lucjan, vi–vii

Donde, Abraham, 26

Dorys, Jerzy, 36

Doublier, Francis, 243

Dreyfus, Alfred, 243

Dubnow, Simon, 184, 188, 215

Dworzecki, Mark, 214

Dzigan, Szymon, 240, 245, 249

Einhorn, David, 226

Eisenberg, Leybl, 176

Eisner, Gustav, 19, 32, 36, 113, 117, 118, 119, 121, 122, 143

Eisurowicz, Borys, 198

Ejgel, J., 232

Elkin, Mendl, 227, 241

Ellenbogen, Chaim Bolek, vi

Elzet, Yehude. *See* Złotnik, Yehude Leyb

Epstein family, 162

Erlich, Henryk, 199

Erlich, Rachel, vi

Erlich, Yitskhok, 76

Erter, Isaac, 5, 6

Fajans, Maksymilian, 3, 4, 5

Farbstein, Joshua Heschel, 175

Faust family, 99

Feldberg, Leyzer, 145

Fenton, Roger, 20

Fiałko, A., 14

Fishberg, Maurice, 15

Fogel, Suzanna, vi

Forbert, Leo, 203, 239, 246, 247

Ford, Aleksander, 247

Franz Ferdinand, 112

Franz Josef, 114

Friedland, Zvi, 237, 242

Friedman, Mark, vii

Friedman, Moshe Daivd, 70

Frischmann, David, 219, 224

Fuks, Marian, 27, 126

Fryshdorf, Hannah, viii

*The names of photographers, studios, collectors and individuals associated with photography are italicized.

265

Tolpin, Moyshe, 107
Tomaszewski, H., 248
Towbin, Mojzesz Mordka, 244
Trunk, I. I., 225
Trunk, Isaiah, vi
Tshortkever rebe. See Friedman, Moshe David
Tunkel, Joseph, 173, 223
Turkow, Jonas, 246, 247
Turkow, Ruth, 245
Turkow, Zygmunt, 234, 238, 241, 245
Tuwim, Julian, 228

Unger, Sholem David, 73

Vanzetti, Bartolomeo, 235
Vilna Gaon, 54, 59
Vishniac, Roman, 32, 33, 36, 51, 52, 53, 55, 72, 75, 81, 84, 96, 149, 156, 158, 167, 168, 169, 176, 199
Vorobeichic, M., 32, 33, 34, 36, 42, 64

Waislitz, Jacob, 241
Waksman, E., 244
Walter, Paula, 237
Warburg, Felix, 123
Warski, Adolf, 187
Warszawski, Adolf. *See* Warski, Adolf
Warszawski, Oyzer, 225
Wawelberg, Hipolit, 163
Wawelberg, Ludwika, 163
Wawelberg family, 162
Web, Marek, vi
Weichert, Michał, 235
Weinberg, Bella, vi
Weinreich, Beatrice Silverman, vi
Weinreich, Max, vi, 215
Weintraub, 16
Weinzieher, Salomon, 129
Weiss, A., 215
Weissenberg, Isaac Meir, 225
Weissenberg, Samuel, 15
Wilson, Thomas Woodrow, 22, 121, 122
Wirgili-Kahan, B., 215

Wiślicki, 109
Witos, Wincenty, 141
Wittlin, Halina, 229
Wittlin, Józef, 228, 229
Wixlowa, Adela, 30
Wizun, A., 14
Wygodski, Jacob, 97

Yelizariants, 244

Zabłudowska, Irena, vii
Zagelbojm, 107
Zajczyk, Szymon, 16, 31, 67, 68
Zamenhof, Ludwik, 212
Zandberg, Yitskhok, 234
Żdżadski, Wacław, 5
Zhabner rebe. See Unger, Sholem David
Zheleznikov, J., 215
Zhitlowsky, C., 215
Złotnik, Leyb Yehude, 18
Żychliński, 145

Index of Places

WITHDRAWN